JB JOSSEY-BASS™
A Wiley Brand

Celebrating Your Nonprofit's Milestones

81 Great Ideas for Planning and Celebrating Milestone Events

Scott C. Stevenson, Editor

WILEY

Celebrating Your Nonprofit's Milestones

81 Great Ideas for Planning and Celebrating Milestone Events

Published by

Stevenson, Inc.

P.O. Box 4528 • Sioux City, Iowa • 51104

Phone 712.239.3010 • Fax 712.239.2166

www.stevensoninc.com

81 Great Ideas for Planning and Celebrating Milestone Events

TABLE OF CONTENTS

TABLE OF CONTENTS

Celebrating Your Nonprofit's Milestones

81 Great Ideas for Planning and Celebrating Milestone Events

 ### 1   Reconnect With Community By Celebrating Company's Anniversary

Celebrating your organization's anniversary is important, whether it is the first or 100th. Acknowledge important milestones and use them as an opportunity to get the community reconnected to your cause.

Several years ago the Animal Protective Foundation (APF) in Scotia, NY, celebrated its 75th anniversary and the organization commemorated it in a variety of ways.

According to Marguerite Pearson, director of communications and outreach, the APF redesigned their logo, the banners in their parking lot and their newsletter to reflect the anniversary. The APF also held special events such as a volunteer appreciation mixer, a charity walk for animals and were able to garner feature articles in local papers.

When planning your anniversary celebration, be sure to consider fresh ideas of how to get the community involved and to shine the spotlight on your organization all year. The APF celebrated in unique and interesting ways, such as putting together a timeline of the organization's milestones for display and burying a time capsule to be opened in 25 years.

With enough planning and a lot of enthusiasm, you can make your anniversary celebrations last the whole year.

Source: Marguerite Pearson, Director of Communications and Outreach, Animal Protective Foundation, Scotia, NY.
Phone (518) 374-3944 ext. 113.
E-mail: pearson@animalprotective.org

 ### 2   Mark Events With Memorable, Show-stopping Features

Pull out all the stops and go for the "wow" factor when planning for a major celebration, says Christian Kendzierski, media relations, office of communications, Mount St. Mary's University (Emmitsburg, MD).

"When celebrating our 200th anniversary, we ordered a cake made by the Food Network's "Ace of Cakes" for our bicentennial party," says Kendzierski.

A staff member from the advancement/development office first suggested they order a cake from the Ace of Cakes bakery and creative studio, located in Baltimore, MD, about 60 miles from campus.

"After some consideration and figuring we only turn 200 once, we thought, why not go for the 'wow' factor of the cake and have them build one of our trademark cupolas?" says Kendzierski. "Lots of people here are fans of the show and were excited about the idea.

"The cake was fairly pricey," he says, "but the press and attention received was advertising you can't buy."

Three feet tall and 18 inches across, the cupola cake — which took 30 hours to complete — took center stage at the anniversary celebration at the Marriott Baltimore Inner Harbor. Alumni, guests, award recipients and local clergy dined on sheet cakes from Ace of Cakes as they admired the centerpiece. The showpiece cake was taken to campus for students to enjoy at a winter dance.

To help designers accurately capture the campus showpiece in sugar, flour and fondant, university staff provided photos of the cupola from several angles and sketches from the communications team.

Not only did the elaborate cake and celebrity status of its makers bring additional attention to the university's milestone, the reality show also assigned a TV crew to cover the party to gather interviews and footage for the "Ace of Cakes" episode.

The TV show "was great exposure for the school and the bicentennial celebrations," he says. In addition, local media coverage of the anniversary celebration included Baltimore newspapers and one TV station, which mentioned the presence of the cake at the event.

Source: Christian Kendzierski, Media Relations, Office of Communications, Mount St. Mary's University, Emmitsburg, MD.
E-mail: kendzierski@ msmary.edu

Created by Food Network's Ace of Cakes team, this confectionery rendition of a trademark cupola took center stage at the 200th anniversary of Mount St. Mary's University (Emmitsburg, MD).

3   Leverage Your Cause's Milestone to Maximize Exposure, Draw Support

Leveraged properly, an organizational milestone can mean media gold and new supporters for your cause. Make the most of your milestone by:

✓ **Holding multiple events year-round that vary in cost, location and formality to include a broad range of people.** For example, members of the Santa Clara Vanguard Drum & Bugle Corps (Santa Clara, CA) celebrated its 40th anniversary with a birthday dinner, spring concert, golf classic and other events.

✓ **Being creative in the ways you include people.** The Drum & Bugle Corps formed a 2007 Anniversary Alumni Corps, inviting former members to perform with current members and cadets during the year.

✓ **Combining multiple milestones.** The ReBuilding Center (Portland, OR) celebrated a 10th anniversary with the opening of new offices.

✓ **Tying your events directly to your mission.** The ReBuilding Center's new offices were built with more than 90 percent reused materials.

✓ **Having a bigger message.** Organizers of a 20th Birthday Year of Celebration for the Make-A-Wish Foundation of Northeast New York (Cohoes, NY) invited past wish recipients to events. These ambassadors — many of whom were by then young adults — helped dispel the common misconception that only terminally ill children receive wishes from the organization.

✓ **Focusing on the future.** Use the milestone to announce a capital campaign or new program, set new goals or break ground on a new facility.

4   Cultivation Idea: Tie Attendee Number to Anniversary Year

If your organization is about to celebrate a milestone year, tie the anniversary year to promotions and special events.

One way to do so is to follow the example of New Beginnings, a domestic violence agency in Seattle, WA.

When New Beginnings celebrated its 30th anniversary the organization encouraged friends and supporters to host individual anniversary parties — "Invite 30 for the 30th" — to benefit the nonprofit organization.

Parties could be organized in any of three ways, according to Zoë Myers, New Beginnings director of development:

1. **Fundraisers** — Hosts' guests were invited to help provide shelter and advocacy through financial support.

2. **Friend raisers** — Guests were invited to learn more about New Beginnings' efforts to end domestic violence.

3. **Collection drives** — Guests were encouraged to bring items (presents) from New Beginning's wish list. The agency even has online gift registries with Target, Amazon.com and Home Depot.

"New Beginnings assisted interested hosts in lining up a speaker, printed materials and tips for hosting a successful party," Myers notes.

Source: Zoë Myers, Director, New Beginnings, Seattle, WA. Phone (206) 783-4520. E-mail: info@newbegin.org Website: www.newbegin.org

5   Celebrate Members in Internal and External Publications

Using internal publications to share member milestones such as a 25th wedding anniversary or 25 years as a valued member is a great way to highlight important events.

Why not take it a step further and publicize these occasions in other community publications as well?

Depending on your budget, you may choose to focus on free community papers when sharing news about members. But if your budget allows, consider taking out an ad in a local newspaper to congratulate members who reach certain milestones.

To keep the costs down, consider taking out an ad four times a year and mentioning all member milestones that have occurred during that time period. The added recognition will not only be meaningful to your current members but hopefully attract interest from prospective members as well.

One added bonus? These efforts will also keep your name fresh in the minds of other community members, including the media.

6   **Celebrating an Anniversary? Give Supporters 'A Look Back'**

Nearly everyone likes looking at old pictures and remembering when.

With that in mind, communications officials at the Lower Cape Fear Hospice & LifeCareCenter (Wilmington, NC) turned a special 25th anniversary edition of its newsletter into a look back at a quarter century of serving southeastern North Carolina.

"This special edition was a way to walk down memory lane and also show our beginnings as an agency and how far we have progressed," says Barbara VanSlyke, communications coordinator at the hospice agency. "Six to nine months before the anniversary, staff from our outreach, communications and development departments met to toss ideas around on how to celebrate our anniversary. Through our internal newsletter, we also asked the agency staff and board members to submit ideas."

Those ideas culminated in the special edition newsletter, which featured:

- An invitation to an anniversary celebration at the hospice facility.

- Personal messages from the executive director and other current and former staff sharing some of their most rewarding memories.

- A timeline highlighting important moments in the hospice's history.

- A list — 25 Reasons Why Lower Cape Fear Hospice & LifeCareCenter is Special.

- Invitations to support the agency through bequests and giving clubs.

- Quotes from patients' families.

- Scrapbook-type pages, including one with photos and 25 words describing volunteers as the heart of the hospice.

Source: Barbara VanSlyke, Communications Coordinator, Lower Cape Fear Hospice & LifeCareCenter, Wilmington, NC. Phone (910) 791-4860. E-mail: Barbara.VanSlyke @nhhn.org

Content not available in this edition

Content not available in this edition

With the theme, "Twenty-five Years of Celebrating Life," a special-edition anniversary newsletter for the Lower Cape Fear Hospice and LifeCareCenter (Wilmington, NC) included, top to bottom: an invitation to a public celebration and a timeline of milestones.

---

 7   **Tie 'Ask Amounts' to Your Anniversary**

Is your nonprofit approaching a milestone such as 10th, 50th or 100th anniversary?

Tie gift requests to that milestone. Here are some examples of how other nonprofits have linked ask amounts to their nonprofits' 50th anniversary milestones:

1. Ask nondonors to make a $50 commitment in honor of your anniversary.

2. Launch a special campaign to raise $50,000 or $500,000 for a special project.

3. Pull together 50 existing donors willing to establish a challenge fund that will match all new and increased gifts for the year.

4. Launch a "Society of 50," enlisting 50 key donors willing to pledge $1,000 or more.

5. Invite past donors to increase their giving by 50 percent, the additional amount to be used for a specific funding project.

8   Milestone Anniversary Commemorated by Completion of New Building

Officials and supporters of The Children's Theatre Company (CTC) (Minneapolis, MN) celebrated the company's 40th anniversary by unveiling its new building with a weekend-long open house event called "Imagination Unwrapped."

The event featured a parade consisting of 11 groups of children and teens from the community, including an honor guard from the Northern Star Council of the Boy Scouts of America, the North Minneapolis Boys and Girls Club 30-piece Drum Corps and several children's cultural drum, band and dance groups.

After opening remarks from company leadership and guest speakers, children from the parade and in attendance pulled on giant ribbons to unwrap the new rotunda and officially open the new 45,000-square-foot building. The new building is home to the McGuire Education Center (four classrooms, a dance studio, a student performance space and the Best Buy Educational Lounge); expanded scenic, costume and prop shops; and the Cargill Stage, primarily for teens and preschoolers.

A musical piece, "Electric Guitar Orchestra," composed by renowned guitarist John King specifically for the organization's grand opening weekend, came to life as it was performed by dozens of Twin Cities' teens on electric guitars. Sir Kenneth Robinson — an internationally recognized speaker on applying creativity and imagination to arts, education, business and life in general — launched the McGuire Education Center.

The weekend also featured opportunities to see all the new spaces on a self-guided tour, sample classes, taste foods from area restaurants and bakeries, dress up in costumes, listen to stories, register for classes and win prizes.

To welcome people to the special weekend, CTC officials sent postcard invitations to all subscribers and single-ticket buyers to their productions, and to a purchased mailing house list, says Rachel Flynn, public relations associate. Ticket holders to dedication-weekend performances received more targeted information and a reminder to come early to experience the open house before the shows.

Two newspaper ads also welcomed people to the celebration.

"We saw a steady stream of people, especially on Saturday," Flynn says. "The parade was well-attended and many of the attendees came through the open house at that time. The event succeeded in introducing constituents to the new space and the programming, many for the first time."

Source: Rachel Flynn, Public Relations Associate, The Children's Theatre Co., Minneapolis, MN. Phone (612) 874-0500. E-mail: pr@childrenstheatre.org.

9   Parking Decals Serve as Membership Badge of Honor

Providing members with parking decals not only makes identifying members easier, but it also can serve as a marketing tool and renewal reminder for members.

"Since we are a land trust organization, the parking decals indicate to us and others using our preserves if someone is a member," says Holly Meeks, membership and special events, Lake Forest Open Lands Association (Lake Forest, IL). "Most importantly, no one is allowed to walk dogs in our preserves unless they're a member, which would only be indicated in the parking area with cars displaying a Lake Forest Open Lands decal."

Providing decals of this kind enables your members to be identified easily by your organization and community members. It's also a great way for members to show their commitment to your organization. "I think people almost view the decal as a badge of honor for their involvement with an environmental organization on a local level. In addition, when non-members see the number of cars with decals parked at the entrance of a preserve, it gets them thinking about the importance of the land, the happiness it brings and the importance of conservation for future generations and hopefully encourages them to support the organization by joining," Meeks says.

Decals can be used for various reasons and convey different messages depending on your organization's growth. "Our logo has become very recognizable through the decals. It also has allowed us to project a special message such as this year's 40th anniversary message. On a more pragmatic note, it reminds members when their membership expires and to expect renewal invoices."

Source: Holly Meeks, Membership and Special Events, Lake Forest Open Lands Association, Lake Forest, IL. Phone (847) 234-3880 ext. 10. E-mail: hmeeks@lfola.org

Content not available in this edition

Lake Forest Open Lands Association's parking decal.

10 Celebrity Emcees Draw Attention to Special Event

Looking for a way to enliven your special events? Include a local media personality as your event emcee.

"Many times when we have world-class exhibitions come in, we will use local TV news celebrities to emcee the opening events/gala and broadcast live from our facility," says Betsy Woods, marketing and media relations manager, Midland Center for the Arts (MCFTA) of Midland, MI. "The result is that we gain more regional coverage from the media to help get the word out about MCFTA and our programs."

"MCFTA has a very strong relationship with our local media (including TV, radio, print and newspaper). All mediums are willing to work with us as far as providing in-kind sponsorships and support," Woods says.

When reaching out to local media with an emcee request, begin with contacts with whom you already have a working relationship. If they are unable to participate, ask them to refer you to a colleague who might be interested. In MCFTA's case, she says, they often contact sales account representatives they know at local stations to connect with media personalities.

In asking local media personalities to participate as event emcees, she says, "We are pretty informal with the local media that we already have good relationships with. If asking someone we don't know very well, we will send a formal letter and a press packet which consists of a CD of images, an overview informational sheet of the exhibit or performance, media preview invite and/or gala invite, etc."

In addition, art center staff follow up with a thank you to all media contacts who participate, whether through a phone call, e-mail or handwritten thank-you note.

Once a media contact is on board to emcee your event, make your expectations clear, Woods emphasizes. "Typically, media personalities will give us a few hours of their time. They will kick off an event by helping promote our silent auctions, raffles, doing live remotes, giving announcements and acknowledgments, and basically keeping the event lively and fun and promoting MCFTA.

"We recently had an exhibit that focused on the cultural evolution of the 1960s and had two well-known radio DJs from an oldies station be the emcees at our kickoff party. They also did a live remote from our building prior to the

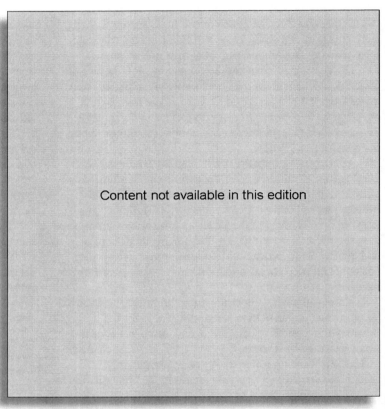

Content not available in this edition

Using local celebrities to emcee events such as a preview party helps draw attention to events for the Midland Center for the Arts (Midland, MI).

party," says Woods.

Having a media personality emcee your event will not only add excitement during the celebration but will increase interest leading up to the event, she says, emphasizing the importance of promoting the special guest in as many ways as possible.

"We will include celebrity involvement on personal invitations, through radio advertising and promotions, print ads, newsletters and our website," Woods says. "It's great for us when the local media personalities get involved and can talk about what we offer to our region.

"People love to be a part of an event where local celebrities attend," she notes, "because many people feel they know them on some level whether it's through hearing them on the radio or seeing them on TV."

Source: Betsy Woods, Marketing & Media Relations Manager, Midland Center for the Arts, Midland, MI.
Phone (989) 631-5930, ext. 1274. E-mail: woodsb@mcfta.org

11 Planning, Preparation Essential to Yearlong Events

Staff at the Visiting Nurse Association (VNA) of the Treasure Coast (Vero Beach, FL) undertook a huge task by planning a year's worth of events celebrating its 30th anniversary. Setting the bar even higher, they sought to meet, recognize and thank every group that helps VNA through those events.

A 30th anniversary committee made up of the communications department, top management and advisory staff members chose to plan several events throughout the year, rather than the two large events that marked VNA's 25th anniversary year.

"We thought having multiple events throughout the year would be a more effective way to involve and recognize more people in our celebration," says Kristine Woolley, community relations manager. "It was a lot of fun and a great learning experience."

Woolley outlines the planning steps committee members took:

- First, they listed groups they wished to target: board members, founders, donors, patients, community, community partners, physicians, employees and volunteers.

- Next, they brainstormed to think up events to recognize and thank each group.

- They developed an updatable plan for each event, including as many details as possible, e.g., date, time, location and budget. They included theme, goals, target audiences, tactics, outline of non-event communications, budget and a timeline.

- The committee started meeting monthly six months before the anniversary year began and throughout it, along with some side meetings, discussing both upcoming events and those that had already taken place.

- The 30th anniversary theme was reflected in everything the community relations department put out that year. Every event was promoted and given to the media separately, but always tied back to the anniversary theme. The 30th anniversary logo was printed on VNA letterhead, added to the VNA logo, put on postcards, invitations, fliers, press releases, newsletter articles, the website, used during interviews and for give-a-ways. More than 30 anniversary-related articles, photos and briefs appeared throughout the year in local media.

Woolley says pre-planning and making adjustments throughout the year were essential. While acknowledging that the year's worth of events required a large amount of time, she notes that the process can be used again: In 2007, the organization celebrated the 25th anniversary of its hospice program; and many elements and ideas from the previous plan were incorporated into the hospice anniversary plan.

Source: Kristine Woolley, Community Relations Manager, Visiting Nurse Association of the Treasure Coast, Vero Beach, FL. Phone (772) 978-5546. E-mail: kwooley@vnatc.com

12 Plan Community Celebration

Will your organization be marking a milestone year? Here are ideas to invite the community to celebrate with you:

- ✓ **Hold a signature party.** Host a public reception and ask guests to sign and decorate a banner or 10-foot poster to display in your organization and feature as a full-page newspaper ad.

- ✓ **Build a landmark.** A major anniversary could be the ideal way to launch a building campaign, be it for a flower garden or concert hall. Offer options for supporters to make anniversary donations (e.g., $100 for name on a plaque, $500 for names engraved on a donor wall brick), scaling upward in proportion to the donation.

- ✓ **Hold a greeting card contest.** Ask supporters of all ages to make cards for your celebration. Display all entries; give prizes for best artwork, content and message.

- ✓ **Make a birthday video.** Invite volunteers, employees or donors for a celebration. Have a videographer interview guests about their roles in your mission. Ask them to sing "Happy Birthday".

- ✓ **Publicize a birthday wish list.** Update and redistribute it or post it online as items are received. Be flexible and creative; include small and large items. Assign dollar values with the option of cash donations.

13 Be Creative When Dedicating New Building

Looking for a unique, media-catching way to dedicate that new building or reveal that recently completed project? Here are two creative ideas to help you go beyond the traditional first gold shovelful of dirt or ribbon cutting.

"At the dedication ceremony for Hollins' new library, we had a line of students and faculty stand from in front of the old library to the new and pass significant books along the line to the new library."

— *Laura Tuggle Anderson, Associate Director, Alumnae and Donor Relations, Hollins University (Roanoke, VA)*

"When we celebrated the opening of the third portion of our new campus center (the middle section joining a newly constructed arena opened in Fall 2006 and a renovated classroom building opened in Fall 2005), we didn't want to have another traditional opening just a year after the hoopla surrounding the new arena, so we had a breakthrough. Our facilities people put pictures of the construction process on a foam core wall, hinged in the middle. The president, along with campus and community dignitaries, were given hammers painted gold,

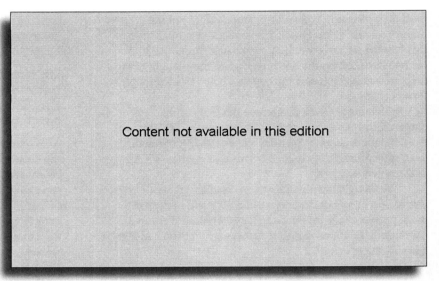

Content not available in this edition

State University of New York at Oswego officials use gold-painted hammers to break through a wall to reveal a new campus center.

and they tapped on the wall, opening the hinged portion to lead everyone through to the newly refurbished area. We also had a presentation thanking donors in the new auditorium."

— *Michele Reed, Director of Alumni and Development Communications, State University of New York at Oswego (Oswego, NY)*

14 Tap Organization's Heritage for a Memorable Anniversary

Is your organization coming up on its one-, 10-, 25- or 100-year anniversary? Are you seeking ideas to create a memorable, crowd-pleasing celebration?

Here are some ideas for kicking off your coming years in style:

- Tap your organization's unique history for ideas. For Minnesota's sesquicentennial, the Washington County Historical Society (Stillwater, MN) held a beer tasting and presentation discussing the state's beer industry, from the first illegal brewery to major companies operating today. Organizers also held a baseball festival in which teams from across the country partook in the game as it was played in 1858, the year Minnesota became a state.

- For a gala event, use a fun theme to keep everyone lively rather than stuffy. For example, for a Hollywood theme, hire celebrity look-a-likes, pass out Oscar award statues

and put eclectic favors on the tables, such as oversized Elvis glasses. You can even pass out ever-popular gift bags full of promotional material and history of your organization.

- The North American XJ Association (www.naxja.org), an organization for off-road vehicle owners, gave away a 1996 Jeep Cherokee for its 25th anniversary. While anyone can give away a car, the members decided to take it one step further — offering an off-road vehicle that was built by the membership itself.

- Sometimes just having a great speaker at your anniversary gala can be enough. The John D. O'Bryant African-American Institute at Northeastern University (Boston, MA) celebrated 40 years with Dr. Randall Pinkett, a Rhodes Scholar, author and businessman. However, Pinkett may be better known as a winner of the reality TV show, "The Apprentice."

15 Make the Most Of Your Agency's Milestones

Is your volunteer program reaching an historical milestone? Take advantage of it by getting some extra publicity.

When the Hospice of Tuscarawas County Inc. (Dover, OH) was approaching its 20th anniversary, Kasey Rippel, provider relations, scheduled a meeting with the local newspaper to publicize the milestone.

That meeting turned into a two-hour interview with a full spread on the organization's history, accomplishments and celebration, as well as post-event coverage with photos and a brief editorial.

Rippel says garnering the media's coverage began years prior by building a rapport with the newspaper (e.g., sending thank-you notes to the reporter following events and referring other businesses to the media outlet).

When publicizing a milestone, Rippel suggests supplying the media with the following information:

- **Organization history.** Talk to key organization officials (executive director, CEO, founders) to gather a detailed history.

- **Major accomplishments.** Rippel says it's important to note milestones from the past and present, as well as mentioning future goals.

- **Stories of people your organization has served.**

- **Meaningful statistics** — Number of people served, etc.

- **Photographs of the organization's progress through the years.**

- **Staff contact information** — Individuals who can serve as potential sources and those who have been with the organization for several years.

"Publicizing your organization's milestones gives you the golden opportunity to educate the public about your services while sparking people's interest to volunteer or donate," says Rippel.

Source: Kasey Rippel, Provider Relations, Hospice of Tuscarawas County Inc., Dover, OH. Phone (330) 343-7605.

16 Encourage Anniversary Gifts

More and more people are celebrating the special occasions in their lives (e.g., weddings, birthdays, etc.) by encouraging their friends and relatives to make a gift to their favorite charities in lieu of personal gifts.

Why not take a more proactive role in encouraging friends of your organization to celebrate milestone anniversaries — 10th, 25th, 50th and others — by inviting their friends and relatives to make a gift on their behalf (as opposed to personal gifts)?

Here are some ways to do that:

✓ Offer a room in your facility for anyone wishing to host an anniversary reception. This gets new people to your premises and allows them to see some of what your organization is all about.

✓ Produce a large supply of preprinted notecards that anniversary couples can include with their invitations saying, "in lieu of a personal gift, we would be grateful if you made a gift to [name of your organization] in tribute to our anniversary."

✓ Offer facility tours to the anniversary couple's guests in conjunction with their open house.

✓ Place the names of all guests, especially those making a tribute gift, on your mailing list for future newsletters and event announcements.

✓ Publicize the event by taking photos and including them in the next issue of your newsletter.

17 Include Membership Milestones On Your Event Calendar

If your organization has an online event calendar, consider including member celebrations such as birthdays and notable anniversaries along with special event listings.

Each January, send out a mass e-mail to membership asking them to let you know of important milestones coming up that year, such as a retirement, 25th or 50th wedding anniversary, etc.

Including these special dates on your online calendar helps staff keep track of and acknowledge them while encouraging members to send good wishes as well.

In addition to including dates on your calendar, include a congratulatory message on your website addressed to the member celebrating a special occasion.

While some members may not wish to have their birthdays or other events listed, many members may appreciate the recognition. What's more, it serves as a free and relatively easy way for you to connect with your members.

18 Plan a Successful Inauguration Ceremony

An inauguration ceremony welcoming a new president is one of the most important events in an organization's lifetime — which can make the thought of planning and executing the event overwhelmingly daunting.

Tom Ryan, vice president of institutional advancement, and Linda Rosenlund, director of special events, Assumption College (Worcester, MA), recently worked together to coordinate the inauguration of President Francesco C. Cesareo. Here, they share tips on how to orchestrate a successful inauguration ceremony:

1. **Start early.** They began planning for the inauguration six months in advance.

2. **Create a planning committee.** Assumption College's inauguration committee made up of 30 people, including the president, met every other week from July through October with subcommittees (operations, other events and inauguration ceremony) involving more people meeting during the in-between weeks.

3. **Do your research.** Ryan and Rosenlund cite two books produced by The Council for Advancement and Support of Education as being extremely helpful during the planning process; "Academic Ceremonies: A Handbook of Traditions and Protocol", and "Presidential Inaugurations: Planning for More than Pomp and Circumstance".

4. **Establish a budget, but leave room for the unexpected.** In Assumption College's case, they chose to invest in a $1,500 generator in case of loss of power.

5. **Give the press access to the new president,** providing information before the event and opportunity then and elsewhere to meet and interview the president.

6. **Have copies of all speeches and other materials in advance.** College staff had a binder at the podium during the event containing all speeches and other scripted information, which was especially helpful to the master of ceremonies.

7. **Make all speakers and presenters aware of time limits.**

8. **Create easily identifiable signage.** Event and directional signs were made for all of the college's inauguration-related events. Indoor signs included at least one sign or banner at each venue that stated "Welcome to Assumption College." Directional signs helped guide persons to their destinations.

9. **Attend an inauguration.** If you haven't planned an inauguration before, attend one so you can see how they work.

10. **Plan for bad weather.** Even though Assumption College's inauguration took place indoors, organizers rented vans to transport guests, purchased umbrellas and took other steps to be prepared to go ahead in inclement weather.

11. **Utilize your students/staff/clients.** Some 35 Assumption College students worked as ambassadors, welcoming guests to campus.

12. **Create action plan charts.** These charts should list all event specifics — cost, responsibilities, etc. — and require all subcommittees to keep up-to-date. Ryan says these were instrumental in not only keeping subcommittees on target, but also helped improve communication between the various committees.

13. **Establish a parking and traffic plan.** Ryan says they used both campus and city police officers. We sent delegates a packet the week before the inauguration containing a map of campus, and a parking pass and instructions.

Source: Tom Ryan, Vice President of Institutional Advancement, Assumption College, Worcester, MA. Phone (508) 767-7000. E-mail: tryan@assumption.edu

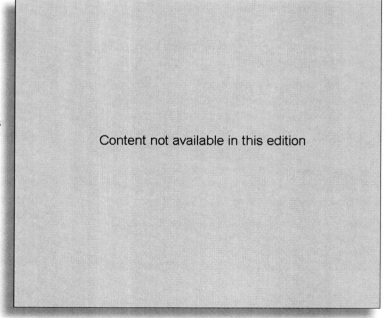

Content not available in this edition

Assumption College Trustee Chair Fred Bayon presents President Francesco Cesareo with the Presidential Medallion at Cesareo's inauguration.

19   Raise Funds While Celebrating Long-time Hero's Contributions

Do you have a special employee or much-respected board member who is leaving or retiring? Use the departure of this well-known person as an opportunity to celebrate the person's contributions while raising money for the cause he or she holds so dear.

In three years, the Autumn Gala for the Botsford Foundation (Farmington Hills, MI) has grown from a quaint event to an extravagant hospital fundraiser while keeping one goal in mind: remembering and honoring special hospital leaders.

Diane Shane, manager of foundation programs and services, says the event grew from an idea by a physician leader — also a foundation board member — for a gala to raise funds and honor the hospital's medical staff. The foundation got involved because the medical staff committee needed assistance with the program/advertisement book and auction.

The straight-forward gala evolved into a way to also honor a medical staff hero when two longtime physicians passed away that year.

"We were raising money in an effort to honor their memory with the naming of the ambulatory surgery suite and the hospital chapel," Shane says of the premiere event in 2006. "The foundation staff decided to ask the medical staff if proceeds from the gala could be used to match the dollars raised for both initiatives."

The result was a $70,000 gift from the medical staff.

In the gala's second year in 2007, organizers recognized one of the hospital's founding physicians, with foundation members asking for gifts in the founder's honor. Attendance grew by 100 guests and raised $125,000 for the hospital's capital campaign.

The 2008 event incorporated the retirement of hospital CEO, Gerson I. Cooper, after 50 years of service with the hospital.

"We thought about holding an independent event honoring this legacy leader, but felt we couldn't support two high-priced ticket events," says Shane. "So the event became the Botsford Hospital Medical Staff Autumn Gala and Gerson I. Cooper Tribute."

Because of Cooper's contacts on state and national levels, Shane says the committee felt comfortable reaching beyond traditional limits to sell tickets and seek sponsorships. They set ticket prices at $275 per person and sponsorship levels at $5,000 to $50,000.

The event included a video about Cooper's life, as well as speakers talking about his leadership and legacy at the hospital and at local, regional and national levels.

Bringing in $500,000, the 2008 event raised more than double that of the first two years combined. Proceeds benefited the hospital's cancer center, says Shane, who notes attendance has also grown steadily, 275 guests in 2006 to 400 in 2007 to 650 in 2008.

Source: Diane Shane, Manager of Foundation Programs and Services, The Botsford Foundation, Farmington Hills, MI. Phone (248) 442-5046. E-mail: dshane@botsford.org

20   Use Construction Period to Point to Progress

If facility construction or renovation is taking place at your nonprofit and you're not inviting the media, donors and others to witness the changes taking place, you're missing a great opportunity.

For most nonprofits, a period of major construction/renovation is an infrequent occurrence. And when it does take place — even if it may be messy — most people will perceive the changes being made as progress. The noise, the construction workers, the chaos surrounding the project are all perceived as steps toward an enhanced environment.

To get the most from your organization's construction project:

✓ Invite small groups of individuals to view the project at various points throughout the construction phase. Think about whether it is to your advantage to mix members of the media with donors or community leaders or target each group separately. Both approaches have advantages.

✓ Pay attention to detail after guests arrive. Depending on your construction project's size and scope, you may wish to make golf carts available for tours. Pay particular attention to safety factors. You may decide to distribute hard hats, for instance.

✓ Have persons present who can point out changes taking place and how those changes will impact those served by your organization.

✓ Conclude the tour with refreshments and brief remarks by your CEO or board chair.

Make it a standard practice to set follow-up appointments with attendees to answer questions or pursue feature possibilities.

Use Milestones, Stats to Grab Public's Attention

You've admitted another patient to your hospital. So what? Unless it happens to be the one-millionth patient. Your domestic violence center recently helped its 1,000th client. Your art center is about to host its 100th exhibit.

Sometimes a milestone or a statistic is all it takes to capture the public's attention. That's why it's helpful if someone in your organization is keeping tabs on data that your office can spotlight when the time is right.

Some examples that might generate a moment in the spotlight include:

- Achievement stats.
- Economic impact stats.
- Historical stats.
- Comparative stats.
- Customer, client stats.
- Days, months or years of operation.

 Honor 10-year Members With Keepsake Gifts

In today's fast-moving society, the 10-year anniversary has become the new 25-year anniversary in the workplace, as well as in member organizations, says Gord Green, executive vice president of Rideau Recognition Solutions (Newmarket, ON). That's one more reason to focus on retaining current employees or members.

Recognition and incentive programs are effective strategic tools to retain and engage valuable human resources, Green says. "On the 10-year anniversary of a member, give the volunteer an award, not a reward.

"An award isn't something you can earn or buy, like a salary," Green says. "In essence, don't pay them. Make sure the award has a high trophy symbolic value."

In other words, award the member with an item whose symbolic value far outweighs its cost, such as a lapel pin, ring, trophy or plaque.

An award doesn't diminish in value. A significant and respectable award can be passed on, and it never ends up in the garbage or on a garage sale.

Have the symbolism of an organization embedded into the award to give it even more value. Use a symbol that is unique and meaningful to your organization.

A true award puts the members in an elite group, which gives them feelings of personal validation and self-worth.

Service awards provide an ideal opportunity to focus on each member of your organization, one person at a time, Green says. Awards celebrate individuals, not just for reaching an anniversary milestone, but for the excellence they bring to your organization every day.

Source: Gord Green, Executive Vice President, Rideau Recognition Solutions, Newmarket, ON. Phone (905) 830-2990. E-mail: sales@Rideau.com. Website: www.rideau.com

 Make the Most of Membership Milestones

Highlighting your membership milestones brings recognition to your organization and your community.

Anthony L. Baskerville, national membership director, Disabled American Veterans (DAV) in Cold Spring, KY, says, "It's critical that we involve our members to get the energy to reach our goals. Without their support, achieving our goals is impossible. Reaching one-million fully paid life members was something DAV members across the United States worked together to achieve. It shows us how successful we can be when we mobilize and that we are a vital, capable organization."

DAV made sure to publicize this membership milestone to reach all members, supporters and the media. "We worked with our communications team to get a cover story article in our magazine, which reaches our 1.3 million members, most of our leaders in Washington and various people who work with veterans or are visiting DAV facilities throughout

the country. We also made sure it was the lead story on our website, where it remained for almost a quarter. And if that wasn't enough, we sent out a national press release," Baskerville says.

Sharing membership milestones reminds your members your organization is committed to success. Baskerville says, "It reminds people we're relevant and alive. It tells our veterans we're not alone. It tells lawmakers we have support in their districts and throughout the country. It shows the American people we're growing. Even though the popularity of veterans' service and fraternal organizations seems to be declining, we're getting bigger. We're using this surge to evolve so we can take in this new generation and give them the care and service we know they've earned."

Source: Anthony L. Baskerville, National Membership Director, Disabled American Veterans, Cold Spring, KY. Phone (859) 441 7300.

24 Recognition Program Celebrates Continuous Membership

Send your members personal cards to mark special anniversaries — and to encourage their renewals.

The Association of Legal Administrators (ALA) of Lincolnshire, IL sends anniversary cards to members celebrating their first and fifth, as well as 10th, 15th, 20th, 25th and 35th anniversaries.

"We recognize only continuous and uninterrupted membership, so this encourages members to be timely in renewing their memberships," says Debbie Curtis, director of membership.

A personal touch enhances the success of the recognition program. "The association president personally signs cards for all individuals with 25 or more years of continuous membership; this is approximately 200 cards," Curtis says. "The notes were of a personal nature and varied depending on whether the president knew the recipient."

They also used postage stamps for mailing the anniversary cards, rather than postage meters, to make them more personal. Approximately 2,500 cards were mailed in 2006 — the project's first year.

Most members gave ALA positive feedback for their postcards. "Members really appreciated the recognition and the fact we took the time to acknowledge their achievement," Curtis says.

Negative feedback came from members who had a break in their service at some point. For example, ALA sent a five-year anniversary card to a member who had been with the organization off and on for 15 years. In those cases, the organization explained its continuous and uninterrupted requirement for anniversary recognition.

"The goodwill created far outweighed the limited negative feedback," Curtis says.

Content not available in this edition

ALA hired a design company to create the cards and matching envelopes. Another company was hired to handle the printing and mailing. "The initial cost per card/envelope was $2 to $2.25, including postage," Curtis says. "This will be lower in future years, since the design costs (included in the card costs) are a one-time expense."

Source: Debbie Curtis, Director of Membership, The Association of Legal Administrators (ALA), Lincolnshire, IL. Phone (847) 267-1388. E-mail: dcurtis@alanet.org

25 Make the Most of Anniversary Milestones

Is your organization about to celebrate an anniversary? Congratulations! Now get to work on ways to tie your fund-raising efforts to the anniversary year.

Here are some suggestions:

- Launch a capital or endowment campaign that uses your organization's anniversary year as its dollar goal (e.g. 25-year anniversary: $25 million).

- Ask for donation amounts that coincide with your anniversary year (e.g., $25; $250; $2,500; $25,000).

- Develop an anniversary-year fundraising appeal that solicits, for example, 25 gifts of $25,000; 250 gifts of $2,500 or 2,500 gifts of $25.

- Launch a new annual giving club for donors who pledge to make generous gifts (e.g., $2,500; $25,000) to your Annual Fund campaign over a five-year period.

- Celebrate donors who have been a part of your organization since its inception or for a certain length of time, such as 10 years, with a letter of recognition and invitation to make a special anniversary gift.

26 Find Attention-grabbing Ideas to Celebrate Milestones

Milestone anniversaries present opportunities to reach out to new audiences throughout the celebration year. Like birthdays, anniversaries — especially those marking significant years such as 25, 50 or 100 — are the perfect time to spread good will and good news.

Here are just a few ideas to do so:

✓ **Form a speakers' bureau.** Your organization likely has several people prepared to give presentations about its past, present and future to service clubs, social and business groups, Chambers of Commerce and schools. Make the most effective speakers available for media interviews as well.

✓ **Launch community outreach programs.** This is an ideal time to begin a service that expands your scope. Venture into job training, preventative health or other areas that coincide with your mission while filling a need.

✓ **Host birthday events all year.** Invite the community to celebrate with you several times during the year through spring marathon walks or runs, a summer concert series and a Founder's Day party with cake and all the trim-

mings. Make events family-friendly to boost attendance.

✓ **Publish an advertising supplement.** Choose a local news or business publication to produce a full-color special edition featuring stories and photos about your history; interviews from longtime employees, board members or volunteers; current goals and activities; and leadership strategies to lead you forward. Invite vendors and others to buy ads. Make sure to print extra copies to distribute after the original run.

✓ **Create an anniversary logo.** Put the logo on all printed materials, billboards and advertising, as well as items available for purchase, like polo shirts, caps, plates, jewelry or bags. Sell them in your gift shop, online or give to new donors or volunteers.

✓ **Celebrate construction.** The timing may be right to announce a construction or landscaping project. Donors may purchase engraved bricks for a special wall or walkway, trees or statues in a peaceful courtyard, or artwork in a newly renovated area of your building.

27 Tell History With Timeline

When an anniversary or milestone calls for creating a timeline, populate it with more than just your organization's accomplishments. Add local, regional, national and/or international events to give historical perspective.

That's the approach that officials with St. Lawrence University (Canton, NY) took for a timeline marking its sesquicentennial celebration, says Mark Mende, Web services director.

"Our goal was to relate highlights from the university's 150-year history and place them in context with other historical events," says Mende. "We tried to make the timeline brief, easy to use and informative; and I think we met all of those criteria."

Fifteen Web pages, each of which captures a 10-year span, interlink to highlight the university's history since its 1856 founding. The timeline parallels significant university

events with those of the world (see sections, below).

St. Lawrence staff and students alike contributed to the timeline, Mende says: "We had a student do all of the research for the content of the timeline.... Then I came up with a design concept. Based on our resources and the amount of time available to accomplish the project, I decided to go low-tech — while it would have been fun to do something like a Flash-based timeline, and we might consider doing that in the future, I think people shouldn't shy away from more low-tech solutions. They might not be as cool, but are often much more usable."

Portions of the timeline are shown below. View all 15 pages at: http://web.stlawu.edu/150/timeline.html

Source: Mark Mende, Director of Web Services, St. Lawrence University, Canton, NY. Phone (315) 229-5955. E-mail: mmende@ stlawu.edu. Website: www.stlawu.edu

Content not available in this edition

28 Visual Theme Intrigues Readers, Connects Them With Organization's History

Creating a visual theme for publications by repeatedly using a familiar image will strike a chord with your readers and serve as a valuable design element.

Oranges and citrus trees are unifying tools for the annual report for Saint Leo University (Saint Leo, FL), says Susan Shoulet, director of public relations. The images also play up the university's history. Founded in 1889 by Benedictine monks, the main campus is surrounded by citrus groves. "I've often heard stories about how the monks sold the oranges to help support the school in lean economic times," Shoulet says. "We knew alumni would connect with the trees and the oranges."

The university's signature colors of green and gold further the citrus grove tradition, says Shoulet, noting that this is the second year the university has used the design theme in the annual report.

"It's more subtle than just oranges or orange trees on each page," she says. "The first thing we did was to create a template with some style rules for the entire publication; color, fonts, and some basic design elements that were to be used throughout the publication.

"When we designed the first report, I knew the use of the orange slices and segments on the financial report page might be a little risky, but since we published the first report, I've only heard good things about the design."

The report goes to all university alumni, numbering more than 50,000, so design appeal was crucial, Shoulet notes. "It has to appeal to alumni who have never set foot on the campus here in Florida, and it has to represent the university as a unified organization," she says.

"We think we achieved that through the annual report's design and content."

Shoulet, who has a graphic design background, came up with the concept of utilizing the orange tree images in the report. The 2006-2007 annual report, designed by an outside freelance designer, and the 2007-2008 report, by the in-house graphic designer, both incorporate stock and original images.

When choosing a visual theme for your publication, choose images that are meaningful to your organization and will resonate with your supporters, Shoulet advises. "Look to the past for concepts and images; look to the future for how you will apply them to the publication."

Source: Susan Shoulet, Director of Public Relations, Saint Leo University, Saint Leo, FL.
Phone (352) 588-8121. E-mail: susan.shoulet@saintleo.edu

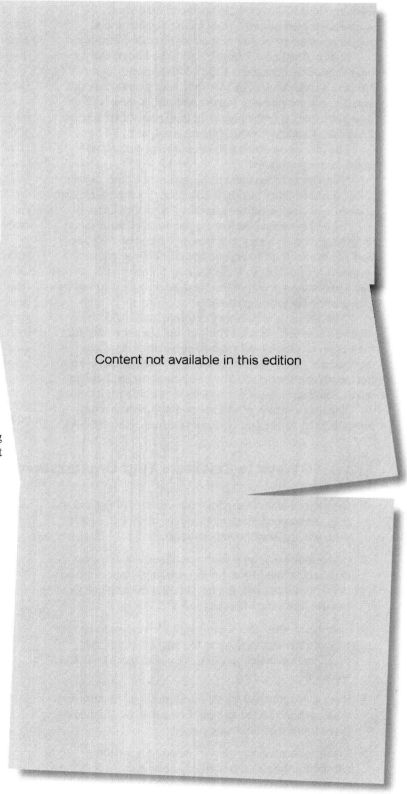

Content not available in this edition

29 University Celebrates 175th Anniversary With Time Capsule

Looking for a striking way to commemorate your anniversary celebration? Create a time capsule and encourage your entire community to join in the festivities.

Staff at Stephens College (Columbia, MO) created a time capsule to mark the college's 175th anniversary in 2008 "to save a little piece of history for future generations and instill in current students, faculty and staff a sense of their own participation in the history of this institution," says Sara Fernandez Cendon, media relations manager.

The idea came about through planning committee brainstorming sessions.

"A member of the committee proposed a time capsule to be 'declared open' during this first celebration of the year, and sealed at the end of the semester," says Cendon.

"The idea seemed perfect for Stephens because we are an institution with a very rich history," she says. "We know how much everyone associated with the college enjoys the materials we hold in our archives, and a time capsule seemed like a miniature version of that, and we thought it would be a nice gesture for future generations.

"We did some preliminary research and found organizations that put a lot of effort and resources into this kind of preservation, and others that had more low-key approaches," she says. "We took ideas from several places, but mostly we were guided by common sense in deciding what should and should not be locked in a safe for 25 years."

The time capsule, which is a gun safe, was given to the college by its Student Government Association (SGA) on behalf of the student body. To boost awareness and involvement of the time capsule project, the SGA also organized a mass e-mail campaign, placed hang tags in residence halls and created a mobile in the student center.

All students, faculty and staff were given the opportunity to place an item in the capsule, either as individuals or as a member of a department. About 100 items were placed inside, including a softball, photographs, brochures, letters, T-shirts, dolls and a necklace worn by the college president at her inauguration.

The capsule is stored in the basement of a campus building and scheduled to be reopened in 2033. "There is a written document that simply states where the key and combination are both stored and when the safe is to be reopened," says Cendon.

"A time capsule can be a really fun project and can help build or strengthen a sense of community," says Cendon. "Keep the amount of time you keep things in a time capsule relatively short — certainly long enough to maintain a sense of discovery when the capsule is reopened, but unless you have the time and resources to prepare items for long-term preservation, such as wrapping in acid-free paper and carefully placing items in the capsule, you're probably better off staying around the 30-year mark."

Source: Sara Fernandez Cendon, Media Relations Manager, Office of Marketing and Public Relations, Stephens College, Columbia, MO. Phone (573) 442-2211. Website: www.stephens.edu

30 10 Ways to Celebrate Your Organization's Anniversary

1. Develop an anniversary logo for widespread general use. (e.g., correspondence, publications, banners, T-shirts, pins, playing cards, bumper stickers, etc.)

2. Commission a limited edition sculpture, painting or sketch by a famous (or local) artist depicting a landmark or the ideals of civic service. Auction the original piece to raise funds for a special project.

3. Coordinate with your Chamber of Commerce to declare a Your Organization Day in the city. Publicize the proclamation in newspapers, TV, radio, businesses and websites.

4. Have a costume ball where guests dress up in attire from your agency's founding year. Feature music, food and decorations from that time period.

5. Create an anniversary flower garden or something similar for the entire community to enjoy.

6. Create an anniversary quilt honoring your years of service. Use each square to highlight a special project.

7. Coordinate an anniversary wine and cheese tasting event. Offer vintages from each year (or decade) your organization has existed and share highlights from your history when introducing a new bottle for tasting.

8. Work with a local auto dealership to emblazon a car with your organizational or anniversary logo. Use it as a pace car at a local racetrack or enter it in a community parade or auto show.

9. Coordinate with local authorities to have a giant anniversary logo placed on a water tower or the highest building in your town.

10. Have an airplane trail a Happy Anniversary banner or sky-write an anniversary greeting at a local air show or similar event.

31   Develop Detailed Plan When Preparing to Celebrate Milestones

When planning a celebration of your organization's accomplishments, Amy Wild, communications and development specialist, The Watson Institute (Sewickley, PA), says it's important to establish a detailed and well-thought-out plan that will distinguish it from others.

Wild says when Watson celebrated the 25th anniversary of its preschool program, LEAP (Learning Experiences: an Alternative Program), the celebration revolved around the widely-recognized success of the program itself.

"It was the first program to integrate children with and without special needs in the United States. Research has been gained as a result of the program and because of its success, many preschools throughout the country have sought out Watson's expertise and consultation when replicating the LEAP model in their own communities," says Wild.

Watson held a three-day celebration, beginning with tours of LEAP's current locations; a reunion party with an informal dinner of current and former staff, program creators and former students; and a conference.

"Because the LEAP model began as a research-based project, Watson decided instead of merely having a dinner to celebrate the 25th anniversary milestone, a conference would also be held, focusing on current trends in educating children with autism, the focus of LEAP's mission," says Wild.

The event brought together those who helped start the program, as well as researchers who gathered data and conducted research in the early days of LEAP, to serve as speakers for the conference.

Source: Amy Wild, Communications and Development Specialist, The Watson Institute, Sewickley, PA. Phone (412) 749-2851. E-mail: amyw@thewatsoninstitute.org

Celebrate Benefits

Wild says celebrating accomplishments can serve many purposes.

1. **Acknowledges and thanks staff.** Celebrating a project's success or a milestone reached by an organization provides the opportunity to thank staff for their hard work and dedication. It can increase employee morale by letting staff know they are valued.

2. **Promotion.** Promoting and sharing the organization's achievement with media and others provides an outlet to share the organization's story, history, mission and future focus. In addition, promoting the agency's accomplishments and staff reaffirms their importance and expertise while offering validity to one's purpose.

Wild says nonprofits may consider recognizing the following milestones: anniversaries; groundbreakings; grand openings; the launch of new programs; fund raising kick-off campaigns; fund-raising goal achievements; staff awards; and partnerships.

32   Bring Your History to Life

When sharing your organization's history, don't limit your efforts to a simple historical timeline. Share the rich history of your organization through a variety of mediums.

Tracy Schario, director of media relations, The George Washington University (GW) of Washington, D.C., offers a few strategies the university uses to share its unique history:

- Leverage your history to strengthen connections with others who may share a common link. "At GW, we utilize both the history of the university as well as the history of our namesake for creative, one of a kind events," says Schario. "In 2004, we commemorated the 100th anniversary of the GW name (founded in 1821 as Columbian College) by planting a six-foot clone of a circa-1785 white ash tree from George Washington's estate at Mount Vernon. In 2007, the inauguration of GW's 16th president featured the same bible that George Washington used for his inauguration."

- Incorporate your history into an annual tradition. "At GW, we celebrate the founding father's birthday each February with a bonfire and cherry pie eating contest."

- Consider joining a parade. Whether it's the U.S. Presidential Inauguration, a sports bowl game, or a local festival, participating in community activities such as a parade, helps raise awareness and establishes a collaborative spirit. GW has participated in two U.S. presidential inauguration parades, including the 1949 parade for President Harry S. Truman and the recent inauguration parade of U.S. President Barack Obama.

By incorporating your organization's history into events you can not only entertain but educate.

Source: Tracy Schario, Director of Media Relations, The George Washington University, Washington, D.C. Phone (202) 994-3566

33 Incorporate Your Mission, Message Throughout Special Year

Does your organization have a significant anniversary coming up? Here's inspiration on how to celebrate the milestone, from the New York City-based ASME organization (the American Society of Mechanical Engineers):

To mark the society's 125th anniversary, ASME held a yearlong series of events, with each event highlighting an aspect of the organization's history, says Diane Kaylor, special projects manager with ASME communications.

"We refocused activities within existing programs and regular events to add significance to the year based on future directions (strategic objectives, topical trends, and identity support), historical ties and public awareness," Kaylor says. All events were sponsored by the companies Marsh and New York Life.

From Model T's to Comic Strips

ASME officials brought public awareness to the anniversary mainly through the selection of specially designated landmarks (e.g., the Ford Model T, Biro ballpoint pen and an early Linotype printing press) by ASME's History and Heritage program, each of which had major impact both to the industry and to the public.

"Two of the five landmark events were held outside of the United States, emphasizing ASME's growing global presence," says Kaylor.

ASME's website published a comic strip series, "Heroes of Engineering," by artist Ron Spellman featuring an engineer or achievement representing the progression of decades from 1880, ASME's founding year, to the present.

"The comic strip received the most attention from the media," Kaylor notes. Check out the comic strips at: http://anniversary.asme.org/comicbook.shtml

Additional Ways to Celebrate
125 Years of Mechanical Engineering

Other ways ASME celebrated the society's 125 years, while using the anniversary to bring attention to the society and the contributions of mechanical engineering included:

- Revisiting significant historical   moments at Stevens Institute of Technology, where   ASME held its first formal meeting, and where ASME's first president

taught and developed mechanical engineering curricula and laboratory.

- Emphasizing its global focus (a major strategic emphasis) through most planned events. For example, ASME was host society for Engineers Week; the word "National" was dropped from its title to reflect the week's increasing global scope; and for the first time, the event's industry co-chair was from a company (London-based BP) not head-quartered in the United States.

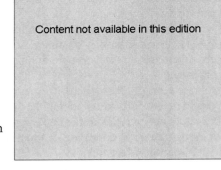

Content not available in this edition

- Holding a main kickoff event, Founders Day, intended to be celebrated locally wherever ASME members met. The event was supported by ASME headquarters through website communications, resource kits for local ASME groups, giveaways, and the introduction of new banners containing the organization's anniversary logo.

- Distributing traditional commemorative medallions featuring the new anniversary logo and tag line "setting the standard," to special recipients. They also distributed a celebratory CD at year-end during the organization's annual Congress.

- Including a yearlong series of articles featuring technological advances, decade by decade, in its flagship publication, "Mechanical Engineering".

Source: Diane Kaylor, Special Projects Manager, ASME Communications, New York, NY. Phone (212) 591-8159.
E-mail: KaylorD@asme.org. Website: www.asme.org

34 Celebrate Employee Milestones

Take the time to celebrate employee milestones and say thanks for a job well done.

One way to bring the office together is an informal celebration. Consider having a monthly meeting that celebrates all employees who have a birthday that month. You can piggyback the celebration with a regularly scheduled meeting and have light refreshments. It's a

chance for employees to interact during work in a casual environment and a great opportunity to praise staff for a job well done.

Ask employees to bring in homemade snacks or take a small collection to cover morning bagels or an afternoon dessert. Staff members will appreciate the recognition and enjoy the chance to connect with each other.

35   Enliven Celebrations With Talent Competitions

Invigorate anniversaries, reunions and other celebrations with talent competitions.

The sesquicentennial celebration for Lincoln University (Lincoln University, PA) included student talent competitions to increase interest among students, says Sam W. Pressley, creative director, Sam W. Pressley Communications (Williamstown, NJ).

Pressley, currently consulting strategic communications coordinator for the university, was its director of marketing and communications at the time of the 150th anniversary celebration.

Under the leadership of President Ivory V. Nelson, the competitions were also created to educate students about their historic university and its significant role in higher education, Pressley says.

They promoted the competitions with campus flyers, in the campus newspaper and in-class mentions.

An 11-member sesquicentennial commission, made up of faculty members, developed the talent competitions that included five categories: essay, oratorical, performing arts, poetry and visual arts.

"Each contest was coordinated by a faculty member who was also a commission member and served as the main contact to applicants," says Pressley.

Hundreds of students submitted applications, using forms accessible on the university's website. Students were asked to include basic contact information including student ID number and class year, and which category they were entering. Pressley says all applications were reviewed by the commission and after thoughtful discussion winners in each category were chosen by a vote.

Winners in each category were announced at the campus celebration that coincided with the university's annual honors convocation, which recognizes its top academic students. Winners were also announced in the student newspaper and on the student affairs and academic affairs websites. Awards and cash prizes were granted to three winners in each category: First place received $1,000, second place, $500 and third place, $250.

Source: Sam W. Pressley, Creative Director, Sam W. Pressley Communications, Williamstown, NJ. Phone (856) 582-3836.

36   Think Unique Dedication Ideas

Planning a building dedication? Find inspiration with these noteworthy ceremonies:

- For the dedication of the University of Washington's Paul G. Allen Center for Computer Science & Engineering, the university produced a commemorative booklet (www.cs.washington.edu/building/dedication/booklet.pdf) with information on Allen's history with the old building (he founded Microsoft with Bill Gates); programs housed in the new building; and profiles of donors.

- Colorado Law School (Boulder, CO) began the dedication ceremony of its Wolf Law Building with a procession from its former home to its new location led by the dean, university president, U.S. Supreme Court Justice Stephen Breyer, University of Colorado regents, faculty and staff of Colorado Law.

- The dedication of the Eric E. Hotung International Law Center Building for Georgetown University (Washington, D.C.) featured videotaped messages from Baroness Brenda Hale (United Kingdom's first female Law Lord); Justice Michael Kirby of the High Court of Australia and benediction by Theodore Cardinal McCarrick, Archdiocese of Washington.

- Massachusetts Institute of Technology (Cambridge, MA) produced a webcast of the dedication ceremony for its Stata Center building (http://web.mit.edu/spotlight/stata-webcast/).

- When dedicating Ball State University's Art and Journalism Building, officials buried a 100-year time capsule that included a Theatre and Dance brochure; Studying Art pamphlet from the Department of Art, copies of the Daily News campus newspaper, coverage of the Sept. 11, 2001 terrorist attack and a CD with the paper's coverage of the events.

- A ceremony for the School of Industrial Labor Relations teaching facility at Cornell University (Ithaca, NY) featured a 150-pound cake replica of the building.

37   **Anniversary Inspires Year-long Celebration, Multitude of Special Events**

If your organization is gearing up for a major anniversary celebration, consider hosting a series of events equal to the number of years you are celebrating.

The year 2009 marked the 50th anniversary of the Natural Resources Council of Maine (NRCM) of Augusta, ME. To mark the occasion, staff and volunteers organized 50 events to celebrate their 50 years of work protecting Maine's environment.

"We decided a drumbeat of events was the best way to keep our anniversary celebration on the radar screen for our members and to engage the broader public," says Allison Wells, senior director, public affairs and marketing.

Planners came up with the concept several years ago and started planning for the 50 events in 2008. They began with monthly meetings for key staff and board members and then increased to every two weeks as 2009 approached. A committee of five people focused on the celebration, with other staff members brought in as needed.

Rather than create 50 brand new events, the committee reviewed the council's existing schedule of yearly events to discuss ways in which they could add a 50th anniversary message to each.

"We flagged certain kinds of events as necessary. Then we set up a spreadsheet of categories like Indoors, Outdoors, Staff-led, Self-guided and also flagged ways to tie activities to nationally or state-recognized special awareness days and weeks," says Wells. "We brought this to an all-staff brainstorm session and made sure we included a wide range of activities, from informal brown-bag lectures to more formal events. We were very careful to make sure we included things that were just plain fun but that fit with our mission and our goals for the celebration.

"Then the real work began, which included sketching out a time line and assigning staff in various roles."

Organizers also tapped into events being hosted by other groups that made sense for the organization to be affiliated with and that would garner significant attention.

"For example, we worked with Bates College (Lewiston, ME) to locate an appropriate speaker for the college's prestigious Edmund S. Muskie lecture," she says. "Our executive director introduced the speaker and both groups promoted the event."

Source: Allison Wells, Senior Director, Public Affairs and Marketing, Natural Resources Council of Maine, Augusta, ME. Phone (207) 622-3101. E-mail: awells@nrcm.org

This 50-year timeline, featured in the Winter 2009 newsletter for the Natural Resources Council of Maine (Augusta, ME) marks significant events in its five-decade history.

Multi-faceted Promotions Buoy Year-long Celebration

To promote a year-long celebration of 50 events to mark the 50th anniversary for the National Resources Council of Maine (NRCM) of Augusta, ME, staff took a multi-faceted approach.

They included an anniversary tagline on letterhead and constantly updated their website to showcase upcoming events related to the celebration. They also used their quarterly newsletter to showcase the accomplishments of the last 50 years with a timeline (see below), promoted anniversary events and celebrated members who take part in the activities.

NRCM staff used online social networking sites such as Facebook (www.facebook.com) and Twitter (www.twitter.com) to get the word out, too.

"We are fortunate to have skilled and creative staff to plan and execute the ideas, which eliminated the need to hire consultants and outside communication firms," notes Allison Wells, senior director, public affairs and marketing.

To encourage people to stay enthusiastic and engaged throughout the year, organizers hosted a raffle for outdoor-related prizes (e.g., kayaks, canoes and lobster bakes). Persons who attended an anniversary event or participated in a self-scheduled event earned points that translated into entry into the raffle.

For more on the year-long celebration, visit: www.nrcm.org/50_years.asp

Content not available in this edition

38   Use Varied Methods to Publicize Milestone Events

A well-rounded publicity strategy will help create a sense of excitement about your events.

To build excitement for the YWCA St. Paul (St. Paul, MN) centennial celebration, Darcie Moore, communications and community relations associate, says they had to employ some new publicity tactics to make the public take notice. Some tactics included designing a custom window graphic for a building located at a busy intersection, installing an inflatable birthday cake on their roof, hanging banners and photographing the executive director and committee members holding a birthday cake.

By using their creativity, the YWCA St. Paul was able to reach a wider audience while sparking community interest. Moore says they were also able to build excitement for the centennial by involving their community and business partners in publicity efforts (e.g., sending out e-mail invitations, hanging posters and working with local papers to obtain free ad placement).

Source: Darcie Moore, Communications & Community Relations Associate, YWCA St. Paul, St. Paul, MN. Phone (651) 222-3741.

39   Preserve History by Recording and Sharing Stories

A great way to preserve your organization's history is to record stories of those you have impacted over the years in the voices of the actual story subjects.

That is the goal of a 100th anniversary project at Florida Hospital (Orlando, FL), says Samantha O'Lenick, executive director. As part of the centennial celebration and as a gift to employees and the community, O'Lenick says, they are collecting and sharing persons' stories about the hospital with the help of StoryCorps™ (Brooklyn, NY).

"StoryCorps is a national oral history project whose mission is to honor and celebrate one another's lives through listening," says O'Lenick. "By recording the stories of our lives with the people we care about, we experience our history, hopes and humanity."

In the project, led by the hospital's five-person community relations team, 108 persons shared their stories in interviews to use with the celebration initiative. Community members and employees of the hospital who were interested in being interviewed were able to sign up on the hospital's website. In addition to posting information on the hospital website, they promoted this effort by running ads on a local radio station.

All interviews were recorded in a sound booth set up in an old furniture store. The community relations team used the store area to create a library of the hospital's history, featuring old nurses' uniforms on display, along with music and banners which featured facts about the history of the hospital, the community and nation.

Refreshments and a comfortable waiting area also greeted the interview subjects.

StoryCorps facilitators were on hand to sit down with interviewees for 40-minute sessions. The goal of the sessions was to obtain stories about how the hospital has touched the lives and hearts of community members.

After each session was complete, participants received a CD copy of their interview, had their photo taken, signed a guestbook and were given a notebook, bookmark and magnet emblazoned with the words: I made history!

All interviews were also sent to the Library of Congress to be archived as part of the StoryCorps project, says O'Lenick. She says they are considering posting a sampling of stories on the hospital website and creating a centennial book featuring the stories as well.

Cost to the hospital — including bringing the StoryCorps facilitators on site to record interviews and purchase the giveaways — was roughly $60,000.

Source: Samantha O'Lenick, Executive Director, Corporate Communications and Community Relations, Florida Hospital, Orlando, FL. Phone (407) 303-8212.
E-mail: Samantha.olenick@flhosp.org

Nonprofit Celebrates Lives by Listening

According to its website, StoryCorps™ (Brooklyn, NY), "is an independent nonprofit project whose mission is to honor and celebrate one another's lives through listening.

"By recording the stories of our lives with the people we care about, we experience our history, hopes and humanity. Since 2003, tens of thousands of everyday people have interviewed family and friends through StoryCorps. Each conversation is recorded on a free CD to take home and share, and is archived for generations to come at the Library of Congress. Millions listen to our award-winning broadcasts on public radio and the Internet. StoryCorps is one of the largest oral history projects of its kind, creating a growing portrait of who we really are as Americans."

To learn more about the nonprofit and its services and fee structure, go to: www.storycorps.com

40 Celebrate Members' Birthdays

Celebrating members birthdays — especially those of children — will serve as a delightful benefit.

At Virginia Living Museum (VLM) of Newport News, VA, parents sign up children, ages 3 to 12, for the birthday club at the admissions desk and online, says Gina Shackelford, membership manager.

"Each month I send out a postcard to all the children with birthdays for that given month. The postcard can be redeemed for a small treat on their next visit," usually a pencil personalized with "Happy Birthday from the VLM" or a themed prize coordinated to the current changing exhibit.

The birthday club, created several years ago, is maintained entirely in-house. Postcards feature a paragraph about options for celebrating birthdays at the museum, along with instructions to bring the card in for the birthday gift.

While Shackelford oversees the data entry, bulk mailings and purchasing supplies, volunteers help label postcards and prepare gifts. Admission desk personnel hand out the gifts and collect the postcards.

Depending on the type of gift bestowed, you may need to create a separate budget to accommodate mailings and gift purchases, she says. She pays about $500 a year for postage and $100 for gifts. For the postcards, she buys cardstock or uses paper left over from special events.

The birthday club, Shackelford says, "is a popular benefit since many members also have their birthday parties here. It has potential for other uses too. For example, the VLM celebrated its 40th anniversary and we invited club members to have cake with us at a special event."

Children's birthday wishes also go out in VLM's quarterly newsletter.

Museum officials promote the birthday club on its website, mention it in all welcome and renewal letters and in the benefit flyer, says Shackelford. She notes that of 1,900 birthday postcards sent, some 371 were redeemed.

Source: Gina Shackelford, Membership Manager, Virginia Living Museum, Newport News, VA. Phone (757) 595-1900, ext. 240. E-mail: membership@thevlm.org. Website: www.thevlm.org

41 Use a Special Anniversary to Generate Additional Publicity

Is your organization marking a special anniversary? Celebrate with a year-long publicity campaign. That's what The National Kidney Foundation of Michigan did to commemorate its 50th anniversary. Lisa Schutz Jelic, director of special events, says weekly planning meetings produced these ideas:

✓ **Logo.** They developed a 50th anniversary logo for the website and all printed materials, including anniversary letterhead used by NKFM for all correspondence. The logo was also featured on holiday ornaments and custom pottery tiles available for purchase, as were silicone bracelets that read "Making Lives Better."

✓ **Kickoff event.** They unveiled the logo and the year-long campaign at a special event. While the event raised just $1,000, it achieved its primary purpose — to raise friends and generate excitement about the organization and celebration.

✓ **Media partnership.** With a public relations firm's help, they partnered with local TV and radio stations and newspaper to provide a specific amount of coverage. Media outlets were identified as NKFM partners on website and printed materials.

✓ **Traveling display.** An 18-panel interactive display that tests the reader's knowledge about kidney disease and its risk factors was available for community events. All costs of the $11,000 display were underwritten by a local sponsor.

✓ **Gala celebration.** Closing the yearlong celebration was the Glitz at the Ritz ball featuring 1950s glamour plus, for six dialysis patients, a Hollywood-type makeover complete with attire, jewelry, hair, makeup and transportation to the event.

Source: Lisa Schutz Jelic, Director of Special Events, National Kidney Foundation of Michigan, Ann Arbor, MI. Phone (734) 222-9800. E-mail: lschutz@nkfm.org

42 **Partner WIth Others Who Share Your Milestone for Joint Celebration**

Are you about to celebrate your organization's 10th, 20th or 100th anniversary?

If you have a milestone anniversary coming up, determine what other businesses or corporations are celebrating that same anniversary. Contact and partner with them to form a joint celebration plan.

A joint celebration provides a way to forge new business relationships, and it might even result in gifts, grants, sponsorships, future cooperative ventures and more.

43 **Renovations Lead the Way to Celebration of Building Dedication**

The opening of your new or renovated facility shouldn't close the doors on recognitions.

A 20th anniversary celebration of the Fletcher Library on Arizona State University's West Campus (Phoenix, AZ) recognized the contributions of the Robert L. Fletcher family and the university's 20 years of service to the growing region, says Steve Des Georges, director of public relations and marketing.

Opened in 1988, the Fletcher Library is named in honor of the Fletcher family in recognition of their gift of land to the ASU Foundation. Proceeds of the sale established an endowment that provides funding in perpetuity to the library.

"The (anniversary) event brought a lot of attention to the library and how long it has been a part of the greater Phoenix metropolitan area," says Des Georges. "Any time you can bring a group of people together to celebrate an accomplishment or a milestone, you build a greater sense of pride for who you are and what you do. It was also a great way to reconnect with the Fletchers and others prominent in the library's founding."

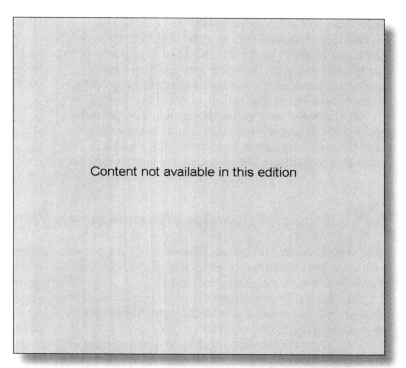
Content not available in this edition

Leading up to the event, three six-foot banners showcasing various stages of library construction were displayed in the library atrium along with posters of staff memories. Photo displays included pictures of library and staff, library construction, dedication ceremony and 10th anniversary celebration. Video displays showed College of Teacher Education and Leadership students interviewing the library's Director Marilyn Myers.

On celebration day, staff gathered for potluck lunch and to view displays of the library through the years, photos of 10th and 20th anniversary staffs, and to share predictions of what the library would be like in 2018. A short program at 4 p.m. included remarks by ASU Vice President Elizabeth Langland, Director Meyers, Associate Librarian Leslee Shell, family representative Bob Fletcher and Gerald McSheffery, the first vice president and architect of the library, followed by cake and refreshments.

"The event was staged in the late afternoon to allow more people to participate, but it was also an informal event that encouraged attendees to visit with others who have played a role in the growth of Fletcher Library and the West campus," says Des Georges.

Invitees included staff of all ASU libraries; staff, faculty and students of the ASU West campus; and the Dean's Advisory Board. About 100 people attended, including the library's entire staff, deans of the colleges and all the campus library directors.

The eight-member anniversary committee included the library director, associate librarians, library administrators, a library specialist, library marketing representative and the events manager for the West campus.

Sources: Stephen Des Georges, Director of Public Relations and Marketing, Arizona State University at the West Campus, Phoenix, AZ. Phone (602) 543-5220. E-mail: Stephen.Desgeorges@asu.edu Janice Kasperski, Associate Librarian, Arizona State University, Phoenix, AZ. Phone (602) 543-8518. E-mail: Janice.Kasperski@asu.edu

44 All-electronic Media Kit Commemorates Anniversary

If your organization is celebrating a significant anniversary or milestone how about creating a commemorative media kit that not only informs the news media about the event, but also educates your supporters and the community as well?

Consider going all-electronic to keep costs at a minimum while capitalizing on the latest computer technology to share the timely information.

Staff with Clarkson College (Omaha, NE) created an all-electronic media kit to commemorate its 120th anniversary.

"We decided to create a media kit for the 120th anniversary to create a greater awareness of the activities included in our celebration." says Melodae Morris, senior director of marketing and public relations. "The goal was to capitalize on another branding opportunity to create a memorable impression in the community with prospective students, parents and alumni."

The kit was created in less than a week using several staple public relations pieces, including a backgrounder, historical timeline and fact sheet, along with a media release and photo, says Kelsey Archer, assistant director of marketing and public relations.

While much of the timeline was already intact, there was some information missing. Morris says the additional information was found in the college's historical archive and in the history book, "Learning to Care", which covers the first century of the college's history. Plus, staff searched through boxes of memorablilia, scrapbooks and photos.

They posted the media kit on the university's website and e-mailed it to media contacts. The only cost involved was that of the staff time needed to create and distribute these materials.

"The response has been exceedingly favorable," says Morris. "The materials are achieving what we hoped to do. We are attracting new alumni membership everyday and so far, the media coverage has been great."

Sources: Kelsey Archer, Assistant Director of Marketing and Public Relations; Melodae Morris, Senior Director of Marketing and Public Relations, Clarkson College, Omaha, NE. Phone (402) 552-6209 (Archer) or (402) 552-6114 (Morris).

45 Museum Celebrates 50th Anniversary With Members, Community

Staff at the Phoenix Art Museum (Phoenix, AZ) had a comprehensive plan to celebrate the organization's 50th anniversary with its membership and community.

Marking the 50-year milestone, the art museum developed a number of events and created specialty items to show its gratitude to its 12,000 members.

Here's how the Phoenix Art Museum communicated to members by honoring the 50th anniversary milestone in the history of the museum:

With an historical written account of the organization:

The "Fabulous at 50" history book was created to showcase the esteemed history of the organization and was unveiled at the museum's annual fundraiser, the pARTy. The compilation was created within six months and contains photos and a historical account of the growth of the museum.

By honoring members with a special event:

The 50th Anniversary Member Celebration, Party Like It's 1959 event was held Nov. 21, 2009, the actual 50th anniversary of the museum. At the event, 30 couples who have been members of the museum for 50 years were honored. Specialty items and offerings from the 1950s era were available to put guests in the time and place when the museum first came to be.

A movie screening featuring "Some Like It Hot" for adults and "Sleeping Beauty" for the younger crowd — both box office hits in 1959, the year the museum opened —

offered a nostalgic retrospective from the era. A barbershop quartet and brass ensemble offered musical entertainment reminiscent of the 1950s. Special architecture tours were also part of the day offering members a detailed physical accounting of the growth of the museum throughout the previous 50 years. Candy, games and toys for children at the event, such as hula hoops, were all geared toward the 1950s theme.

With an event honoring major donors and members:

Major donors and Circles of Support members attended a special exhibition opening reception for the museum's 50/50: Fifty Gifts Celebrating Fifty Years exhibition. This exhibition was the unveiling of more than 300 new pieces acquired by the museum in honor of its 50th anniversary.

By offering a public celebration to the greater Phoenix community:

The Phoenix Art Museum not only created membership events to mark this major milestone, but also created a public celebration to coincide with the Downtown Phoenix First Friday event that features special exhibits by area art galleries and museums. The free Friday night fiesta offered the museum a way to share its anniversary with the public.

Source: Tammy Stewart, Membership and Visitor Services Manager, Phoenix Art Museum, Phoenix, AZ. Phone (602) 257-2124. E-mail: Tammy.Stewart@phxart.org

46 Anniversary Lends Itself to Celebrating, Wooing Major Donors

When staff and supporters of the University of Southern California Thornton School of Music (Los Angeles, CA) began planning for its 125th anniversary two years ago, they began to think of every conceivable way to capitalize on the anniversary — and the number 125 — to attract gifts.

"Our message was that it may be our 125th anniversary, but that this was about building the next 125 years, and that takes resources," says Robert Cutietta, dean. "We decided early on to get everyone on board that our message was about building our future. We weren't ashamed that our future included a need for money."

They planned concerts with 125 in the opus. They designed gifts with 125 in them, soliciting a $1.25 million gift, eight $125,000 gifts, and encouraging alums to increase their $100 gifts to $125 in the spirit of the school's 125th anniversary. Over the course of the 125 days of celebration, the university hosted lectures, concerts, or some type of event every literally every day, says Cutietta.

"We planned a lot of high-profile events for people who give, which has provided many opport-unities to showcase our donors," he says. "The campaign was very successful and a lot of fun. Everyone got into it."

Thirty-one days into the 125 days of celebration, the school held a celebratory dinner and concert that attracted 700 alumni and donors. "We wanted to hold our first large event fairly early into the celebration to show donors the kind of publicity the campaign would get," says Cutietta. Each gift was announced individually, followed by a two-three minute performance tied to the gift, e.g., if the gift was made to the piano program, a student played a short piano piece.

"Donors loved it," he says. "The event attracted more interest from prospective donors. Alums who hadn't been back for years made gifts of $1,250 instead of the $125 gifts we had asked for because they were inspired by the 125th anniversary."

Halfway into the 125-day celebration, organizers had raised $2.5 million, all from gifts that had the number 125 in them or were multiples of 125. Two of those gifts were matching gifts that are now being used to encourage additional $125 gifts, says Cutietta.

The celebration concluded with an anniversary formal gala dinner.

The cultivation and solicitation of major donors were done almost exclusively in person. No written proposals were used. "My wife and I invited one or two couples to dinner, and small groups of donors were invited to a special dinner before certain events," he says.

Alums received three mailings over nine months. The first alerted them of the 125th anniversary celebrations. The second announced the launch of the celebration and invited them to return to campus for anniversary-related events. Neither of the first two mailings included a solicitation. The third mailing included a specific ask.

No printed material was produced specifically for the campaign. Instead, 125th anniversary logos were added to existing materials. School officials created gifts instead, including crystal glasses and computer jump drives with the 125th anniversary logo.

The 125 days of celebration provided numerous opportunities for media coverage, including a full-page spread in the LA Times, as well as articles in targeted music publications. "We did very focused announcements about different programs at the school that would be attractive to specific publications," Cutietta says. "For example, we talked about jazz gifts to the jazz world and piano gifts to the piano world."

The keys to their success were starting really early with the planning and deciding early on what their message would be, says Cutietta: "Our focused, simple message has really captivated people. We also got everyone on board internally first and hired an outside firm to help keep us focused. It helped to have an outsider who doesn't know anything about the internal politics and limitations involved."

Source: Robert Cutietta, Dean, USC Thornton School of Music, Los Angeles, CA. Phone (213) 740-5389.
E-mail: MusicDean@Thornton.usc.edu

47 **10 Ideas to Host Successful Grand Re-opening Event**

If your membership organization is preparing to unveil new member benefits, new giving level structures, a new location or new logo, make the most of this news by hosting a grand re-opening.

Here are 10 ideas to get the most mileage out of your significant addition or change while celebrating current members and encouraging others to join:

1. Choose what type of event will work best for your organization and your community: An open house? A casual picnic? A formal dinner? A community educational forum?

2. Consider offering the event at two or more different times to allow guests a casual daytime option with light luncheon fare and a more business-attire evening event complete with a social hour, appetizers and cocktails.

3. Invite all guests from your organization's original opening, all current members, lapsed members, city/county/state officials, the news media and new members of the community.

4. Offer reporters a behind-the-scenes tour or other ex-clusive access a few days before the event to generate publicity — and traffic — on your big day.

5. Create a business-to-business grand re-opening offering special discounts or trial memberships to other business professionals in your community.

6. Work with organizations aligned with your goals to showcase all resources and organizations in your region.

7. Ask local notables to speak on behalf of your organization. Include long-standing members, especially those well known in your community, to share their experiences by way of a short presentation during the event.

8. Prominently feature the new aspects of your membership. Have on hand new brochures and fact sheets that highlight what's new about your organization and provide details about your membership base.

9. Offer a trial membership with an expiration date to get more potential new members crossing your threshold.

10. Always have membership staff on hand to answer questions about your new offerings and enroll members.

48 **Opera Celebrates Golden Anniversary By Giving Back**

Vancouver Opera (Vancouver, BC) is celebrating its golden anniversary by giving back to the communities that have supported it for the past 50 years.

In partnership with the staff of Vancouver-based resource leader Goldcorp, Inc. —which made a major gift to the opera through a three-year sponsorship — the opera's artists, staff, volunteers, supporters and board members will provide 10,000 hours of volunteer service to various charities from July 1, 2009 to June 30, 2010 through the opera's Community Connections volunteer service program.

In the first month of the program alone, they banked more than 1,500 hours, says Christopher Libby, the opera's managing director.

"The Vancouver Opera Board and staff thought that giving back to the community was a great way to demonstrate our thanks for 50 years of support," Libby says. "Everybody throws a gala for their anniversary (as we will), and we thought this was a great way to demonstrate that the opera and its fans contribute back to the community in a myriad of ways outside the opera house."

Through the effort, Libby says they hope to support other local charities while showcasing the opera's offstage contributions to the community, fostering new relationships between opera supporters and local charities and inspiring others to do likewise.

Opera representatives approached Goldcorp about the sponsorship gift through a member of the opera's board, Steven Dean, who arranged the initial meeting with Goldcorp leadership. Libby says they chose Goldcorp because of its long history of community engagement in the areas it operates.

"Mr. Dean offered to make a contact as a fellow mining industry executive," he says. "Plus, we thought our golden anniversary might have special appeal to them (because of the company name). Mr. Dean went to the extra effort to arrange his attendance via cell phone despite being on a mining trip to Argentina at the time of the meeting."

Libby and staff are getting the word out about the program through press releases, e-mail blasts, its Web page (www.vancouveropera.ca), its blog (http://vancouveropera. blogspot.com/), Twitter (www.twitter.com/VancouverOpera), Facebook (www.facebook.com/vancouveropera), YouTube(www.youtube.com/user/vancouveropera) and promotions through the charities supported by the effort.

Source: Christopher Libby, Managing Director, Vancouver Opera, Vancouver, British Columbia, Canada. Phone (604) 331-4824. E-mail: clibby@vancouveropera.ca

49   **Anatomy of a Year-long Sesquicentennial Celebration**

Officials at Berea College (Berea, KY) knew they couldn't give justice to 150 years of history in a week- or month-long celebration. So they devoted 12 months to Berea's sesquicentennial with the theme: "Celebrating 150 Years of Learning, Labor and Service."

From a homespun fair that kicked off festivities to a summer alumni reunion, the year was ripe with opportunities to draw the media in and share stories about Berea, says Timothy Jordan, director of public relations.

Here, Jordan shares strategies and challenges of a year's worth of news:

Was your year-long sesquicentennial celebration a community relations dream come true, in terms of having so much going on to share with the media?

"Yes, particularly since we had a wide range of events and activities that were of interest to many different outlets, mainstream and niche media."

What was your media strategy for getting coverage of all these events?

"Once we finalized all the dates and details for the sesquicentennial events, we first considered the target audience for each event. Some events were designed for only an on-campus audience, some were for college alumni and some were for the public. Next, we developed a media matrix, listing every potential media outlet for each event. All of the public events were assessed as to the best media format, such as broadcast and print. Then, based on the media format, we conducted a brainstorming session to list all possible media outlet targets, which we prioritized on criteria: their circulation numbers; demographic profiles of their readers/viewers; and geographic coverage areas and how well those matched our alumni and donor constituencies. Then we developed a schedule noting the production deadlines and scheduled the timing of our pitches and releases accordingly."

How did you execute that strategy?

"Once we developed the media matrix, we prepared a timetable to coincide with the lead times required by various media outlets. Since some of our national media targets have lead times of six months or more, we began our contacts with them well in advance of the actual start of the sesquicentennial year. The timetable guided our production and distribution of media materials."

What advice can you share for media coordinators at nonprofits looking for media coverage of milestone events?

✓ **Plan and prepare well in advance.** "In Berea's case, planning began in earnest three years before the start of the sesquicentennial year," he says.

✓ **Anticipate what the media will want and cater to the needs of their industry**. "This may mean having broadcast-quality stock footage for television outlets, and hi-resolution images on disks for print media," he says.

✓ **Enlist as much support as possible from administrators, co-workers, staff and volunteers.** "They may know other media contacts or be able to open doors for you," Jordan says. "Successful events typically are the products of many hands."

✓ **Look for media opportunities beyond the obvious outlets.** "Your local newspaper and television station are likely mainstream targets, but also look for specialty media outlets," he says. "Your event may be appropriate for, and even receive more coverage in, arts, education, entertainment, business and other niche venues."

✓ **Determine what the real story is**. "It may be less about the event and more about the organization behind it," he says.

✓ **Share your media successes with your constituents in a timely manner.** "Be sure to inform all of your internal audiences, such as administrators, co-workers, board of trustees and others about media stories," he says.

Source: Timothy W. Jordan, Director, Public Relations, Berea College, Berea, KY. Phone (859) 985-3020. E-mail: tim_jordan@berea.edu

50   **Celebrating Members' Milestones**

What do you do when a member has been with your organization for five years? 10 years? 25 years?

Don't let those milestone anniversaries slip by without a word of celebration. At a minimum, send members a personal note whenever their memberships hit a milestone. It lets them know you recognize and appreciate their long-standing affiliation with your organization.

51 **Groundbreaking Ceremonies Highlight Donors, Spark Interest**

Groundbreaking ceremonies can spark community and media interest in your construction projects. They also provide an opportunity to highlight your generous donors.

Staff with University of Pennsylvania School of Veterinary Medicine (Philadelphia, PA) host a groundbreaking when they begin construction on a new building.

"One important purpose is to publicly recognize donors who make the building possible. It also lets everyone, including faculty, staff and students, know that a major change is coming to the campus," says Gail Luciani, executive director of public relations. "What's more, a groundbreaking ceremony makes a great bookend with the grand opening or dedication ceremony at the conclusion of construction."

When planning a groundbreaking ceremony, Luciani says, having the appropriate equipment and personnel on hand is imperative. This includes shovels to stage a real ground breaking, and key persons designated to officially break ground and pose in photos. They generally ask the building's donors to pose with shovels for photos.

Have a large sign with the name of the building and those involved (architects, etc.) and an illustration of the finished building. These elements recognize those involved and help people visualize the finished facility while providing a great backdrop for a photo, says Luciani.

Major costs involved in groundbreaking ceremonies consist of shovel rental, tent rental and creation of event-specific signage. Consider purchasing such equipment if you plan to hold ground breakings frequently.

For a personal touch, Luciani says, purchase an inexpensive shovel and spray paint it gold or silver, or use the colors featured in your organization's logo.

Source: Gail Luciani, Executive Director of Public Relations, University of Pennsylvania School of Veterinary Medicine, Philadelphia, PA. Phone (215) 898-1475.

Unique Features Draw Media, Groundbreaking Crowds

Hosting groundbreaking ceremonies for every new construction project, staff with the University of Pennsylvania School of Veterinary Medicine (Philadelphia, PA) know what works to draw valuable attention from both the news media and the community, says Gail Luciani, executive director of public relations.

For a groundbreaking for a new critical care center, named after a donor's son who had recently passed away, Luciani says they sent media advisories to local news media beforehand. "We were very pleased with the turnout, which was approximately 70 percent of the 100 invited guests."

Any steps you can take to set your groundbreaking ceremony apart will certainly attract more attention, she adds.

For instance, Luciani says, "for the Vernon and Shirley Hill Pavilion ground breaking, we had a search-and-rescue dog dig a plastic dog bone with a message inside it out of a pile of sand and take it to the university's president, who was speaking. The dog was the hit of the day."

52 **Past Meets Future in Milestone Conversation**

Ever wonder what the voices of the past would say about the current state of the organization they helped to create? What if you could capture some of those words of wisdom at your special event?

That was the case at the University of Texas (UT) School of Public Health (Houston, TX), when the school celebrated its 40th anniversary with a gala dinner and half-day symposium, says Rebecca Bower, communications specialist.

The dinner featured a conversation with current dean Roberta B. Ness and Charles LeMaistre, former UT system chancellor and president emeritus of the University of Texas M.D. Anderson Cancer Center (Houston, TX). LeMaistre was instrumental in identifying the first dean of the UT School of Public Health and locating the school in Houston at the Texas Medical Center. The symposium also featured past deans recounting their history and several faculty members looking at where they believe the school is headed.

"Our school has six campuses across the state of Texas, so it isn't very often that all of the leadership gather at one event," she says. "This was a learning and sharing experience for most people. Students who attended the symposium were also able to learn from wonderful stories about the innovative and visionary history of the school that we often forget to elaborate on now."

Source: Rebecca S. Bower, Communications Specialist, The University of Texas School of Public Health, Houston, TX. Phone (713) 500-9019. E-mail: rebecca.s.bower@uth.tmc.edu

53   Trumpet Your Organization's Achievements in Tough Times

Heralding your highest achievements is a surefire way to garner positive attention while reminding internal audiences how vital their support is to your continued success.

"In the midst of serious budget constraints, trumpeting your organization's achievements becomes even more critical," says Sharon R. Hoggard, director of communications and marketing, Norfolk State University (Norfolk, VA). "If an accomplishment impacts the entire university, our constituents and the community, we develop a full public relations plan to tout the accomplishments among all of our audiences."

Hoggard and staff use a varied approach to publicize university accomplishments, including sending news releases to local and regional media, as well as science and technology magazines and industry publications. In addition, they promote accomplishments internally in the university magazine, newsletter and daily e-mail blast.

"We also promote accomplishments on our message marquee located just outside of the administration building," says Hoggard. "The marquee shows the time and temperature and a variety of accomplishments and upcoming events."

For instance, she says: "The university has recently earned an accreditation for our engineering programs. We have and will spend a considerable amount of time, energy and talent telling the world of this accomplishment. We are currently preparing an announcement about the accreditation that will be sent to our competitors, businesses, colleagues and other higher education institutions."

In addition to the usual media outlets, "it is extremely important to publicize major accomplishments to our competitors because we want them to know that we are not standing still and that we are current, vibrant and continually changing and growing to meet the demands of our own students and possibly their students, too," says Hoggard.

Follow any restrictions or guidelines that relate to the acknowledgement and how and when you publicize your news, says Hoggard, noting that the university must follow set guidelines from each accrediting body on how it announces each respective accreditation.

Some accomplishments may warrant more publicity than others, she adds.

"The communications team determines the level of publicity for an accomplishment based on its impact on the university community. Those accomplishments that have the greatest impact — ability to raise the university's image in the region, state or nation — will get broad public relations strategies for promotion," says Hoggard. "For really special achievements, we sometimes develop announcements that are mailed out to local businesses, other higher education institutions and colleagues."

> *"It is extremely important to publicize major accomplishments to our competitors because we want them to know ... that we are current, vibrant and continually changing and growing."*

Sharing successes with internal and external audiences reminds them of the strength of your organization and provides your staff with another reason to be proud of their combined efforts, she says: "The accomplishments of one individual, one department, one student, one faculty member is the accomplishment and success of us all. So we devote much attention, time, effort and other resources to promoting the university's services, programs, academics and its people."

Source: Sharon R. Hoggard, Director of Communications and Marketing, Norfolk State University, Norfolk VA. Phone (757) 823-8374.

54   Crazy About Reading Read-a-Thon Helps Celebrate Anniversary

When the Aspen Hill Chapter of the Montgomery County Friends of the Library (Rockville, MD) was looking to celebrate the system's 50th anniversary, members decided the most appropriate way to do so would be with a 24-hour Read-a-Thon, says library manager Paulette Burt. "At first everyone thought it was crazy," remembers Burt, "but as it started to become a reality, we had a lot of people who wanted to participate."

Held on the main floor of the Aspen Hill library, the event went from noon Friday to noon Saturday. "We put a comfortable chair and lamp on a platform and each reader would sit in the chair and read," says Burt.

The public was invited to come listen to readers from every part of the community including children, state senators and a best-selling author. Readers ages 11 to 70 read varied works, from poetry and Shakespeare to the Declaration of Independence.

Source: Paulette Burt, Library Manager, Aspen Hill Community Library, Rockville, MD. Phone (301) 871-2094.

55   **Centennial Timeline Returns College to Founding Principles**

When staff and faculty at Reed College (Portland, OR) began considering options for marking the college's centennial anniversary that will take place in 2011, they outlined a number of different projects designed to help the Reed community appropriately celebrate and preserve the institution's history.

One idea that is proving to be most useful and popular is an interactive centennial timeline, displayed prominently on the college's website.

Jennifer Bates, director of public affairs, says the timeline not only informs their audience of the college's goals, mission and history of the college, it creates a lasting digital archive of the items in the school's special collections.

The visually driven timeline has been a hit among the many college audiences, Bates says: "People seem to enjoy the site and like being able to learn about and see images from our founding years. They also enjoy learning that the college is still true to its founding principles."

While it has been a success, Bates says it required a significant amount of work. A subcommittee worked with an outside design firm to make the timeline a reality. Sections and topics were determined by that committee, with the actual narrative being written by alumnus. Special collections and public affairs worked closely together to edit, organize and post the content.

In the end, the timeline ended up being a two-phase project. The current site that focuses on the college's founding years was launched in January 2009 in preparation for the start of the college's centennial campaign. The second phase of the website will launch in January 2011 to coincide with their centennial year.

Bates says dividing the timeline into two distinct projects helped with the workload. "By choosing to focus on the first few years of the college for this first site, we significantly reduced the amount of content. We focused on telling the

institution's story, and included as many of the supporting documents we could find."

See Reed College's centennial timeline at: http://centennial.reed.edu/

Source: Jennifer Bates, Director of Public Affairs, Reed College, Portland, OR. Phone (503) 777-7289.
E-mail: jennifer.bates@reed.edu.
Website: http://centennial.reed.edu/

Make Time for Challenges When Creating Timeline

Creating a project such as an interactive online 100-year timeline can be especially challenging because the project is so new and labor-intensive.

But that didn't stop officials at Reed College (Portland, OR), who created such a timeline in anticipation of the college's 100th anniversary in 2011. See the interactive timeline at: http://centennial.reed.edu/

Jennifer Bates, director of public affairs, says the two most significant challenges of the centennial project were: 1) outlining the framework for the first phase of the timeline while keeping the second phase in mind; and 2) presenting information to two very divergent audiences — the Reed community, which is very familiar with the institution, and an external audience that may know very little about Reed.

How did they overcome those challenges? Communication.

Bates says Reed officials held many meetings to discuss the challenges and ways to overcome them.

Another important factor, she says, was allowing a great deal of lead time for discussions and implementations.

---

56   **Four Tips to Plan an Anniversary Celebration**

Does your organization have a milestone anniversary on the horizon? These four suggestions will help you plan a winning celebration:

1. If it's not too late, start planning two years out. That way you can have a series of special events that take place all year long.

2. Start digging into your past early. What you discover about your organization's history may provide creative planning ideas. Scout your archives. Talk to the oldest

living individuals who were associated with your agency way back when.

3. At a minimum, form a single planning committee, and if time/resources permit, form a more structured steering committee that oversees several subcommittees. Expanded volunteer ownership of your anniversary will ensure its success.

4. To come up with the resources required to pull off a red-letter event, get sponsors to underwrite portions of it.

57 Host Employee Recognitions to Honor Those With Milestones

This year, host a recognition event for your employees. That's what officials at Bridgton Academy (North Bridgton, ME) have done for 12 years.

Lisa Antell, director of marketing and communications, says the casual atmosphere at the annual employee recognition dinners brings staff together to celebrate the end of the school year and honor those celebrating milestones.

They hold the event the Monday after graduation in the school dining hall.

"This event closes the academic year that, at a boarding school, is exhausting, and provides a rare opportunity for the entire community — faculty, administrators, maintenance and housekeeping staffs, and families — to come together, relax, and take a moment to remind each other of how much we appreciate each other," says Antell. "This is especially true for people who don't cross paths normally, such as those who work at night or early morning."

The headmaster and human resources director plan the event. Sodexho Marriot, the school's food service provider, prepares a buffet with choice of steak, chicken or fish entrees with sides, salad, dessert and coffee. Bottles of wine grace the tables.

As the dinner portion of the evening winds down and coffee is served, the headmaster begins award presentations.

Employees celebrating a milestone anniversary — five, 10 and so on — are honored, as are staff who are retiring or moving on to another organization. The headmaster says a few words about each employee. Honorees may say a few words as well. Each staff member being honored receives $10 per year of service. A printed program, designed in-house, lists employees being honored.

To get the word out, marketing staff send all employees invitations two weeks prior to the event. The invitation is produced in-house, placed in in-house mailboxes and posted around campus.

The dinner cost about $1,450 and drew some 50 attendees.

Source: Lisa M. Antell, Director of Marketing and Communications, Bridgton Academy, North Bridgton, ME.
Phone (207) 647-3322, ext. 208.
E-mail: lantell@bridgtonacademy.org

58 Multimedia Website Celebrates College's Anniversary

In October, Wheaton College (Wheaton, IL) launched an interactive, multimedia website to celebrate the college's 150th anniversary. The website takes you on a virtual journey from the college's founding in 1860 to the present day.

Elisa Leberis, director of Web communications, says the interactive site allows the Wheaton family, who are spread out across the globe, "to really have a piece of the college they can take with them and enjoy anywhere". A timeline featuring video and sound clips, photos from the archive and historic documents arranged by decade is the core of the site.

The website concept came out of planning sessions for the sesquicentennial. Leberis says the creative team began with two main goals. To create a site that would engage people and touch alumni who think of themselves as ordinary. From there they turned to Design Kitchen (Chicago, IL), an agency known for creating interactive Web experiences, to make their website wish list a reality.

Design Kitchen proposed the multimedia timeline. "It's smaller than what we initially thought we wanted, but so much more flexible than we had ever envisioned", says Leberis. The kickoff team began collecting data in April of 2009. They combed through the archives for every photo, video and sound file they could find. An alumni email blast also secured several of the initial stories featured in timeline. Leberis adds, "We had a 1961 graduate who e-mailed back to tell us about a centennial album he put together for Wheaton. With a little digging we found it, and it is now a part of the timeline and can be downloaded."

Now that the site is up and running, alumni can submit their stories and photos to the timeline through a special link. Submissions generate an automated response and are reviewed by the marketing staff before being included on the site. While the bulk of the site will continue to grow throughout the years, the "Alumni Snapshot" tab will serve as a photographic time capsule. Alumni are being asked to send in a photo before Homecoming 2010. The photo will be added to the graduate's location on the map and serve as a "day-in-the-life" anniversary snapshot.

Source: Elisa Leberis, Director of Web Communication, Wheaton College Marketing & Communication Department, Wheaton, IL.
Phone (630) 752-5566. Email: elisa.m.Leberis@wheaton.edu
Website: http://150.wheaton.edu

59 Notable Figures Tie the Past to the Present

Finding a natural fit between your organization and a notable historical figure — whether that be a founder of your organization or someone instrumental in influencing your mission — can allow you to draw attention and historically mark special events within your organization.

Calvin College (Grand Rapids, MI) was named for theologian John Calvin, who was born in 1509. The college celebrated the 500th anniversary of its namesake's birth with events throughout the year, from conferences to on-campus events to formal and less-formal ceremonies.

Dedicating an entire year to celebrate Calvin's birth benefited the college in many ways, says Phil de Haan, director of communications and marketing.

Here, de Haan answers questions about the year-long celebration:

How does connecting to a notable figure of the past amplify an event?

"History is important, but history is especially important at a place such as Calvin College, which was established in Grand Rapids in 1876, and which takes its name from a famous theologian who was born in the 1500s. Taking the time to celebrate today what is lasting and worthwhile about events and people from long ago is a way for a place like Calvin to understand its past and also look ahead to the future. Former Calvin president William Spoelhof had an expression he liked to use about Calvin's responsibilities to past, present and future. He said we needed to be 'grateful to our ancestors, faithful to our heirs.' Connecting an event to a figure from the past is a good way to do that — to recognize those leaders who came before us as we educate and empower the next generation."

By celebrating John Calvin's birthday, did you generate excitement within the college's community?

"In the summer there are fewer opportunities on a college campus for people to come together. Although we offer some summer school classes at Calvin, the majority of our students are not here during the summer months. So having something like a celebration of John Calvin's birthday allows people to get together, to enjoy some cake and punch and to catch up a little. This year we added a short video to the celebration which put a little different twist on things and gave people another reason to laugh and have some fun."

By making this connection to the college, did it draw more media attention?

Content not available in this edition

"We gained media attention as a result of the event, including a nice NPR interview that the director of our center for Calvin studies did, but it really was not planned or intended solely as a media event. Media coverage was a side benefit. In addition we gave the event some of our own coverage on our Calvin website (www.calvin.edu), including posting the video on (the online video sharing site) Vimeo (www.vimeo.com), creating a photo album and more. We also posted it to our Calvin Facebook page (www.facebook.com/CalvinCollege) and our Calvin Twitter feed (www.twitter.com/calvincollege)."

What's your best tip to another organization who wants to connect a notable figure to a current event to draw more attendees or attention?

"Look for places to connect that are authentic and that make sense for your organization."

Source: Phil de Haan, Director of Communications and Marketing, Calvin College, Grand Rapids, MI. Phone (616) 526-6142. E-mail: dehp@calvin.edu

60 Consider Webcam to Illustrate, Celebrate Buidling Progress

Do you have a major building project under way or on the horizon? Engage donors and potential donors in this exciting process to keep them involved and aware of the value of their support.

A webcam helped capture the ongoing construction of the Bob and Shirley Hunter Welcome Center at Abilene Christian University (Abilene, TX).

"The webcam was a unique opportunity for us to connect donors to the project as well as those who have an interest in keeping up with developments on campus," says John Tyson, director of development. "It helped our friends and donors keep up with their investment and remind them of how their funds were being used."

Before construction began, staff mounted a webcam to the university's campus bell tower and began shooting images of the construction site.

The webcam takes eight pictures per minute. Images are stored on a server and then uploaded to the university's website where visitors can click on a still image of the construction to view the live webcam (www.acu.edu/aboutacu/map_acu/webcam.html).

Images on the website are refreshed every 60 seconds.

Kevin Watson, who oversees construction projects on campus, says the webcam will stay up for the duration of the project.

When construction is completed, he says, they can edit the images into a high-speed video that shows the building, from groundbreaking to finish, in about three minutes — a useful resource when talking with donors and potential donors.

The 57,000-square-foot facility will be home to admissions, alumni relations, The ACU Foundation, the Center for Building Community and Career Center.

Sources: John Tyson, Director of Development; Kevin Watson, Administrative Services; Abilene Christian University, Abilene, TX. Phone (325) 674-2659 (Tyson) or (325) 674-2363 (Watson). E-mail: tysonj@acu.edu or watsonk@acu.edu

---

How a Webcam Works

The webcam capturing the construction of the Bob and Shirley Hunter Welcome Center at Abilene Christian University (ACU) of Abilene, TX is wired into the campus network, says Arthur Brant, director of networking services. The webcam works like a still camera, automatically taking and saving eight pictures a minute.

"The camera has Web server software that allows it to take and store pictures, which a second intermediate server can grab and store," says Brant. "The pictures on the university's website (www.acu.edu/aboutacu/map_acu/webcam.html), taken from the intermediate server, are refreshed every 60 seconds."

The webcam can be set to take as many as 30 pictures a second (full-motion video) to eight pictures a minute.

"We chose to go with a lower per-minute capture so as to not overwhelm our servers," he says. "We began taking pictures in December 2007 and are expecting 12 months of construction. At eight pictures a minute, we are taking 11,520 pictures in a given day and 4.2 million pictures by the end of the construction period. That many pictures can take up a lot of storage space."

Brant says they are storing all the pictures from the webcam so that they can create a nonstop-motion video capturing the entire project, start to finish.

Webcams cost $800 to $1,000 depending on the quality of the images captured, says Brant. ACU's mid-quality camera cost about $1,000, plus the cost of a wide-view lens.

"For our purposes we wanted a middle-of-the-road camera," says Brant. "We aren't trying to do full-motion videos. We were more interested in giving people the online experience of a webcam."

Source: Arthur Brant, Director of Networking Services, Abilene Christian University, Abilene, TX. Phone (325) 674-2930. E-mail: branta@acu.edu

---

61 Profile Employees to Commem0rate Anniversaries

When employees reach major milestones (e.g., 10, 20 or 30 years of service), consider profiling them in your publications or on your website. Include a brief staff-written article along with a photo and words of thanks for his/her commitment.

Another option: Share a list of questions with the employee, then publish the responses in a Q-and-A format. Ask about the person's career, what he/she loves about the work and the cause, favorite memories, funny anecdotes or the role he/she played in a milestone moment. Your internal and external audiences will enjoy learning more about your organization and your dedicated colleagues.

62   Formal Plan Leads to Successful Open House

Preparing for an open house? Establishing a well-defined plan and designating committed staff members to execute that plan will help lead to a successful event.

Wheaton Franciscan Healthcare (Glendale, WI) held an open house to premiere the new facility, Wheaton Franciscan Healthcare – Franklin (Franklin, WI).

Jennifer Garbo-Shawhan, director, communications and publications, Wheaton Franciscan Healthcare – All Saints (Racine, WI), says the goals of the open house were three-fold: "To introduce the local communities to their new hospital; to have a chance for current and future patients to meet and greet physicians and staff; and to create excitement about the services and care the facility offers through fun, interactive activities."

Planning began four to six months prior to the event. A committee of 10, including a group leader, was created to handle all the details. The committee began with monthly meetings, switching to weekly as the event drew nearer.

Planners also kept local law enforcement up to date during the planning process to ensure that all legal requirements were being met.

A master planning grid kept track of the planning process. Garbo-Shawhan says the master plan featured the following column headings:

- Activity (invitations, parking, catering, rentals)
- To Do (listed specific tasks for each activity)
- Who (is responsible)
- Status (updated prior to and after each meeting)
- Comments (important notes/details)

As the planning process started to take shape, specific roles were assigned to committee members, including deadlines for each task, and updates were made to the plan by the group leader.

When planning an open house, keep in mind number of guests expected and amount of space and time needed to satisfy visitor curiosity, she advises.

For the Wheaton event, Garbo-Shawhan says, "each guest was given a visitor guide when they entered the building. To keep the crowd moving, we developed a self-guided tour route that would allow the visitors to see most of what the facility had to offer and optimized crowd control.

"Ropes and stanchions guided people throughout the facility and even the elevators were internally operated to keep the guests moving to each floor efficiently," she says. "Special activities were planned at various points along the tour to offer breaks from walking and to thin out the crowd."

Special activities included mini massages, a teddy bear clinic for children, refreshments, prizes and giveaways.

Based on past open house experience, the planning committee arrived at an estimated attendance figure, anticipating 5,000 visitors. Using the turnover rate of the parking lot, the number of giveaways handed out and the number of door prize slips filled out they estimate actual attendance was 6,000 to 7,000 visitors.

Source: Jennifer Garbo-Shawhan, Director, Communication & Public Relations, Wheaton Franciscan Healthcare – All Saints, Racine, WI. Phone (262) 687-3806. E-mail: Jennifer.Garbo@wfhc.org

Content not available in this edition

---

63 Turn Celebrations Into Fundraisers

Sometimes a simple celebration offers an excellent opportunity to raise funds. Just ask officials with Merced College — Los Banos Campus (Los Banos, CA).

The organization commissioned a 25 X 7 foot ceramic mural focusing on the history of the Los Banos community and placed it in the campus' central meeting location.

"The main purpose was to have an incredible piece of artwork in the lobby of the new campus to welcome our students and visitors," says Karen Wiens, dean. "The goal was for the project to pay for itself and generate a few extra dollars to put towards landscaping and other unmet needs."

People can purchase a 6 X 6 inch ceramic tile border piece for $500 each and have their name, business name, service group name or a loved one's name hand-painted on the tile. Wiens says donors have the option to pay in installments of one, two or four payments.

Wiens says the project's goal is to raise $49,000, resulting in a $20,500 profit.

Source: Karen Wiens, Dean, Merced College — Los Banos Campus, Los Banos, CA. Phone (209) 826-3431. E-mail: weins.k@mccd.edu

---

64 Anniversary Idea

Is your organization about to celebrate a milestone anniversary? Use the anniversary as an opportunity to invite support. One university celebrated its 70th anniversary by promoting gifts of $70 and $19.32 (the year of its founding). The two-choice option convinced many non-donors to contribute.

---

65 Identify Member Milestones

Are you missing publicity opportunities that can draw positive media attention and help your member numbers increase? Be sure to include member milestones as an additional way of garnering needed attention. Some examples might include:

✓ Signing up your Xth member.

✓ Recognizing all founding members.

✓ Recognizing the Xth member to do something.

✓ Publicizing member anniversaries such as 5- and 10-year observances.

Also, be sure to ask your members to share their significant milestones with you. Example: Northwest Entrepreneur Network (Bellevue, WA) — www.nwen.org

---

66 School Incorporates Birthday Celebration Into Fundraiser

If your organization is approaching a milestone, use that as an opportunity to generate even more gifts for your annual fund. That's what officials at Louisville Collegiate School (Louisville, KY) did in celebrating the school's 90th birthday.

"We held an all-school (K-12) birthday assembly on the day of the school's founding with a student parade by grades depicting decades by dress and/or theme," says Jeanne Curtis, director of development. "Historical school facts coupled with events of the world, state and local interest throughout the past 90 years were presented in a humorous and poignant program by our upper school drama students.

"To celebrate the milestone throughout the year, we used the 90th birthday theme of giving gifts to Collegiate. In addition, we devised the 90th Birthday Club, and it's been a huge success."

To be part of the birthday club, says Curtis, persons need to make a new or increased gift of $90.

A $30,000 challenge gift from a foundation energized donors to meet the challenge within four weeks with some 210 donors joining the Birthday Club — 5 percent of everyone who was solicited wanted to join in that first month.

All 90th Birthday Club members were listed in all school publications, on the school's website and elsewhere.

"This has been the most fun, happiest annual giving campaign I've ever run, been part of, or heard of," says Curtis. "Everyone loves a birthday party!"

Source: Jeanne Curtis, Director of Development, Louisville Collegiate School, 2427 Glenmary Avenue, Louisville, KY 40204. Phone (502) 479-0340. E-mail: jcurtis@loucol.com

---

67 **Host A Dedication Event That Attendees Won't Forget**

While a major building or renovation project can be grueling, everyone agrees it is something to celebrate. By hosting a stand-out dedication event, you not only show off all of your hard work, you also make a positive impression that will benefit your organization in countless ways.

So where do you begin planning a memorable dedication event?

First, come up with a wow factor, says Andrea Wyn Schall of A Wynning Event (Beverly Hills, CA), one of Southern California's premiere event planners and author of "Budget Bash - Simply Fabulous Events on a Budget". Whether it is through a unique invitation, a special feature at the event or the entertainment, your event must leave people feeling like they have experienced something special.

In addition to working behind the scenes at the Screen Actors Guild (SAG) awards, Wyn Schall's event-planning business has helped numerous nonprofit agencies through the years. Her best advice for dedication events? Come up with a theme and roll with it for everything from the invitation to the party favors.

One popular theme for evening dedication events, she says, is to go Hollywood with lounge-style seating to make people feel like they are in an upscale club.

Another feature that drew oohs and aahs from attendees at a recent event was a large ice luge used to dispense drinks. A fusion of ice sculpture and drink dispenser, the large-scale ice block contains a banked ramp with two channels set in it. A drink, typically alcoholic, is poured from the top of the channel, chilling as it makes its way to a glass at the bottom. To add even more punch, Wyn Schall says, they renamed the martinis that came out of the luge after some of the organization's high-profile board members and donors.

For more family-friendly events, Wyn Schall suggests coming up with a feature or entertainment that reflects the mission of the nonprofit. For example, have an artist create a mural that represents the organization in the facility. During the dedication, have the artist on hand to discuss the art piece with attendees as well as media.

You can get more mileage out of the mural concept by creating postcards, posters and stationery featuring the art piece to give as commemorative gifts or offer for purchase.

Winning Invitation Tips

One of the most important tasks when planning a major event such as an open house for your new facility is designing invitations that will get the people to the major event.

Andrea Wyn Schall, professional event planner with A Wynning Event (Beverly Hills, CA), shares three tips to make your invitation stand out and create a healthy buzz about your event:

1. **List board members or high-profile people associated with the fundraiser or dedication event on the invitation.** Even if someone is unfamiliar with your organization, they may be personal or business associates with those people and will show up at your event to support them.

2. **Don't ignore the power of e-mail and social media to spread the word about your event.** Create an e-vite and have your board members e-mail them out to everyone in their address books. Or have them post the e-vite on their social media profile. Wyn Schall says that if each of your 10 board members has 100 friends, you've opened yourself up to 1,000 more people potentially.

3. **Get creative!** Is there a unique way you can deliver the invites? Some special way you can package them? The invitation is the first impression of the event and you want it to stand out.

And when it comes to entertainment, Wyn Schall says that it is not always in your best interest to spend money to bring in a big-name person. Instead, focus on something that is pertinent to your organization. For instance, if your nonprofit works with kids, have them come in and perform a dance number or a song at the dedication.

Source: Andrea Wyn Schall, Event Planner, A Wynning Event, Beverly Hills, CA. Phone (310) 279-5114. E-mail: andrea@budgetbashbook.com

 68 **Reach Out to New Donors With Commemorative Gifts**

Since non-donors are more likely to donate toward something special, look for celebratory opportunities to invite support: your nonprofit's 10th, 25th or 50th anniversary, the retirement of your longtime CEO and so forth.

If you're celebrating an anniversary, for instance, invite gifts of $1 for each year your organization has been in existence, and direct those gifts toward a funding project that would appeal to first-time donors.

Choosing a funding project that attracts the community's attention and makes people feel good about giving (e.g., a healing garden or indoor aviary) can boost your chances for attracting fresh support.

69   **Make Use of Anniversary Postcards**

Is your organization about to celebrate a milestone anniversary? Search through old photographs for images that would work as postcards. Add brief descriptions on the back side and share the postcards with your supporters in these and other creative ways:

- Offer a set of postcards as a premium to those who make contributions at a set level.

- Use the postcards to announce special anniversary events throughout the year.

- Invite your employees to use them throughout the year for correspondence — personal notes to donors, vendors, clients (students, patients, members) and others.

- Sell sets of the postcards in your bookstore or gift shop or through your website.

- Offer postcards in gift bags to honorees at your anniversary/milestone celebration.

70   **Major Milestone? Consider Hosting a Media Day**

A media day allows you to invite a large number of local media to your facilities and provide an ideal platform to share an important announcement or development.

Dan Jorgensen, former director of public relations and assistant to the president currently serving as adjunct professor for journalism and public relations courses at Augsburg College, (Minneapolis, MN) explains.

"We held a media day to announce a major new scholarship program, Scholastic Connections, to serve students of color and to help offset a hurtful racist letter-writing campaign by one of our alumni. As we learned more about what our alum had been doing, there was a strong sense that something needed to be done in response and that we should create a positive response."

That response? Hosting a media day focused on creating a positive situation out of a hurtful series of events. Specifically, college officials organized the media day to show the media that:

1. While one alum was obviously racist in his attitudes and actions, the college itself was far from it, and faculty and staff were working tirelessly to prove so.

2. The student body was very diverse and students of color were treated with dignity and respect, and playing key leadership roles on campus.

3. Staff and faculty were striving to find ways to make the student body even more diverse, and setting up the Scholastic Connections fund to provide scholarship support and alumni mentors to students of color was a crucial step in that process.

"The Scholastic Connections program was created as a counter to the hurtful things our alum had been doing, and it was officially announced to the media when they came to campus," says Jorgensen. "Because of the lightning-rod effect created by our alum, there was a lot of interest by the media in getting lots of questions answered. Having a day like this gave them an open campus in which to meet the president and minority neighborhood leaders who came to join in and talk about their relationship with the college, and to talk freely with students and faculty about their experiences."

Augsburg's media day led to extensive media coverage by four TV stations, public and news radio stations, major newspapers plus several community and minority newspapers including the *Metro Lutheran* newspaper. Coverage led to two national stories — one by the Associated Press and one by The Chronicle of Higher Education — which, Jorgensen says, "gave Augsburg high marks for the Scholastic Connections program and the college's response to our alum."

A committee spent a month planning the media day, says Jorgensen.

"The committee was made up of the media/PR team and several other staff in the Department of Public Relations and Communication. We also had a couple of alumni, including Syl Jones, whose idea it was to create Scholastic Connections. Syl conducted the opening press briefing and was also available to talk about the issues."

If considering a media day, "Don't be restrictive in where the media can go and what they can do. If you're inviting them to your organization's facilities, make them feel at home and let them talk to people openly and candidly," he says.

Source: Dan Jorgensen, Former Director of Public Relations & Assistant to the President; Judy Petree, Media Relations Manager; Augsburg College, Minneapolis, MN. Phone (612) 330-1176. E-mail: jorgensd@augsburg.edu or petree@augsburg.edu

71 Pull Out All the Stops to Celebrate Milestone Events

When your organization celebrates a significant anniversary, celebrates a major milestone or experiences some other unprecedented special event, you want as many past and present supporters, donors, clients and new friends to be there as possible.

Here are some ways to help persuade those beyond your local constituents to attend.

✓ **Double check contact information.** Be sure long-distance supporters are receiving your mailings. Consider creating a special invitation or even a folder for them containing brochures about your newest programs and services, as well as new attractions in your city that they may not have seen.

✓ **Involve key players, attendees in planning activities.** Contact key long-distance supporters for their thoughts on associated programs, speakers, parties and outings that would appeal to them and others who have moved out of your area. Ask if they would be willing to chair or coordinate one of them.

✓ **Create and issue distinguished achievement awards.** Recognize several individuals who have been instrumental to the success of your organization through the years, regardless of where they live. If they agree to travel to receive the honor, friends and fellow supporters may follow suit. (Be sure to invite persons within the honoree's circle of influence to boost attendance, interest and publicity.)

✓ **Announce plans in an online blog.** The Internet is the perfect vehicle for keeping supporters across the globe informed of your activities. Update it frequently and encourage all interested parties to post and reconnect with other supporters. Let enthusiasm build over a period of weeks or months as plans are finalized and others announce their plans to attend.

✓ **Offer travel and lodging discounts plus opportunities to socialize with other travelers.** Finances may be an issue for some who would otherwise love to travel to your location to help you celebrate. Visit with a travel agency to develop an all-inclusive package with airfare, hotel and car rental, and even tickets to your event. The ability to budget and pay for the expense over several months may make the difference. Boost the enticement factor by adding in a breakfast, cocktail hour or other gathering for the long-distance crowd that includes exclusive opportunity to rub elbows with your CEO, board president or keynote speaker.

72 Create a Time Capsule to Celebrate Significant Events

Dedicating a new or renovated building is just one type of special event for which you might consider creating a time capsule. Other events include celebrating a milestone anniversary, launching a major program or expanding your services to a greater geographic region.

A time capsule creates a built-in option for a special event 25 or 50 years down the line as the next generation unearths the treasure to see what memories are stored inside.

A time capsule event can also be an opportunity to generate media coverage while setting up opportunities for related media events. To make the most of your time capsule dedication event:

✓ **Stage a group photograph.** Gather volunteers, staff, board members and supporters to pose for a photo forming the numbers in the year you plan to open the capsule. Include some small children and babies who might be at the opening ceremony.

✓ **Hold a sneak preview of capsule items.** Invite media to film a display of photos, newspapers, clothing, technology or copies of speeches, and announce the time and date of the ceremony to encourage attendance.

✓ **Give a demonstration on how to assemble a time capsule.** Special considerations like proper materials, items to avoid because they easily deteriorate or become unusable because of technology changes may be an interesting way to draw newcomers to your organization.

✓ **Predict the future.** Gather supporters to write about their predictions for the year the time capsule will be opened. Host a coffee or lunch where the correct type of acid-free papers and inks are provided. If your time capsule is small, have a contest to determine which ones will be included, but save the others for a display both at your facility and online.

✓ **Host a children's activity.** A coloring contest, a joint mural scroll project that will fit into the capsule or donations of a favorite toy for children of the future can be fun ways to involve an audience who might still be here to see the capsule opened again.

73   Build Anticipation WIth Online Countdown Clock

Counting down the days until a major transition or event is a great way to generate excitement among internal and external audiences. Placing an online countdown clock on your website will expose this unique publicity effort to an even wider audience.

In October 2008, Malone College became Malone University (Canton, OH). To mark that milestone, officials posted a countdown clock on the home page of their website. The clock started ticking on May 4, 2008 and counted down the days to the transition, right down to the second.

The countdown clock idea came up in meetings of the transition committee, a group of 20 people charged with planning all events and programs relating to the transition, says Suzanne Thomas, director of university relations. "We saw (the countdown clock) as a way to build excitement while communicating the upcoming change."

The creation of the clock was a collaboration between the university's Web content manager and In The Round (Canton, OH), the firm that handles the design of the university's website. The clock did not require any updating or maintenance on the part of the university.

"We were under a time crunch because our transition team came up with the countdown clock idea and wanted it implemented as soon as possible," says Andrea Finefrock, Malone's Web content manager. "I sat down with In The Round and told them exactly what we wanted; the creative team came up with a mock-up of the clock within two weeks.

"We wanted something that fit within our template of the home page where photos are normally located," and matched existing webpage colors, Finefrock says.

They used the countdown clock along with other publicity efforts and community events designed to create excitement about the name change.

"The countdown clock has proven to be an effective tool used to keep an important event front and center before our publics," says Thomas. "Perhaps the most interesting response came when one of our faculty members was visiting China and a gentleman there said, 'Oh Malone College, only 62 days until you become a university!'"

Finefrock says she heard from faculty members at other colleges as well as vendors who noticed the clock.

The public relations officials note that a countdown clock could also be utilized to announce other major developments, such as the announcement of a new president, unveiling of a new mascot or the opening of a new building on your campus.

Source: Suzanne Thomas, Director of University Relations; Andrea Finefrock, Web Content Manager; Malone University, Canton, OH. Phone (330) 471-8239 (Thomas) or (330) 471-8514 (Finefrock). E-mail: sthomas@malone.edu

An online countdown clock tracks minutes until Malone College becomes Malone University (Canton, OH):

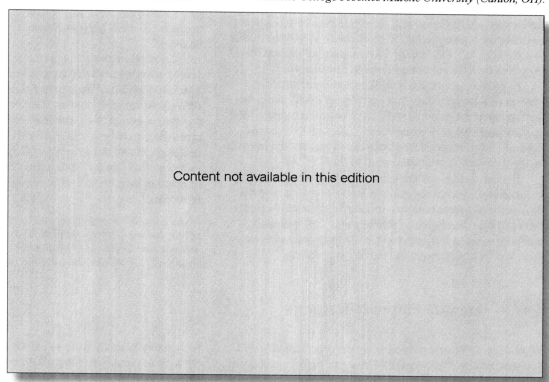

Content not available in this edition

74 Host a Successful Open House

Hosting a successful open house requires forethought, enthusiasm and a capable team.

Amy Blackford, assistant director of the enrollment center, Indiana University-Purdue University Indianapolis (Indianapolis, IN), shares her approach for hosting a memorable open house.

"I try to approach our open house events like a party. The people coming are our guests, and everything has to be perfect," Blackford says.

"One thing I have learned is that in addition to the climate and culture of an institution, the physical landscape sends a message," she says. "I have often found myself climbing tables five minutes before opening to wipe away overlooked cobwebs. It is important that every aspect of your open house is addressed."

When planning an open house, having a dedicated team of staff members who are excited about and invested in creating a successful event is key.

"What we have found to work quite successfully is to embrace the team approach," Blackford says. "We have an overall program coordinator who serves as the touch point for all parties involved, but we also engage others to take on parts of the process. For example, we hire an event coordinator to negotiate with outside vendors and manage the rentals; we have one staff person to take care of guest evaluations, another to take care of check-in tables, another to schedule staff, etc. It truly takes a group of dedicated people to own the process and make it successful."

Eye-catching materials will grab and maintain the interest of your attendees, not just at your open house, but leading up to the event as well. "It is essential to have solid publications and good promotions," she says. "This will depend on the intended reach of your event, but the larger it is, the broader the terms you need to think of."

In open houses for the university, Blackford says, "We use a series of pieces for our two larger events: a save the date postcard (sent about two months in advance), a poster (sent to libraries, churches, schools, etc.), an invitation mailer (giving an in-depth look at the program and is sent three weeks in advance), and the day-of program."

Timing is Everything

One major element in creating a successful open house is to make sure you plan your event for a time that is convenient for the majority of your target audience.

To help minimize conflicts and maximize attendance, be sure to make note of any major event dates that may coincide with your planned open house, advises Amy Blackford, assistant director of the enrollment center, Indiana University-Purdue University Indianapolis (Indianapolis, IN).

"Think about what external factors might impact attendance: SAT or ACT test dates, band practice, basketball games, homecoming," says Blackford. "A student may have every intention and desire to attend your event, but if their band practice or basketball game coincides with your event, they will not be available to you."

Blackford also stresses the importance of fostering a sense of excitement among all those involved in creating an open house. "It is essential to have the buy-in and excitement of your entire community. If everyone is not on board — or not as invested as you need them — then their energies won't be there."

Creating an environment that appeals to your attendees is also essential to the event's success. To achieve this, Blackford advises, "Rather than thinking about what is most convenient for staff or what seems to make most sense from an internal perspective, you have to think about what would serve the guests best, and then work backwards to put the necessary mechanisms in place. It can be a challenge, but the only way that you can have a truly comprehensive, guest-oriented event is to look at it through the lens of what serves them best."

Source: Amy Blackford, Assistant Director, IUPUI Enrollment Center, Indiana University-Purdue University Indianapolis, Indianapolis, IN. Phone (317) 278-6241. E-mail: ablackfo@iupui.edu. Website: visit.iupui.edu

75 Identify Future Milestones

What does 2010 hold for you and your organization? Will you reach a significant year of service or perhaps recognize a major goal regarding your fundraising or volunteer hours served?

A nonprofit's key milestones — anniversaries, anticipated achievements and more — can creep up and pass by before you know it. To avoid that happening to you, take the time to identify future milestones. Prepare a multi-year calendar and list key dates you plan to celebrate or publicize to be sure they get the attention they deserve.

Then set the planning mechanisms in place to recognize and celebrate these significant events.

76 Seven Ways to Celebrate Your Facility Dedication

A new building or addition is reason to celebrate, and the dedication of the structure provides opportunities to invite the public to see your mission in action.

The best time to begin planning your building's dedication is well before construction is complete. There are even pre-dedication events that can enhance community interest.

Here are seven ideas to create a personal, meaningful dedication event:

1. **Hold a topping-off ceremony.** Keep abreast of construction progress, and determine a time when the final structural beam will be placed. Before the crane raises the beam, have board members, key staff and supporters on hand to autograph and date the beam with permanent paint pens. Invite as many persons as construction notice permits to build interest in the approaching dedication.

2. **Plan an open house of both the new and existing facilities.** Have all departments participate by having their areas ready for visitors. Have displays, refreshments and tour guides throughout the buildings to ensure all areas are seen and traffic flow is smooth.

3. **Provide live music.** Small ensembles of singers, children's orchestras or soloists performing in various locations will draw visitors from area to area.

4. **Use photo and brochure displays near exits.** Include attractive photos of organization activities or an historical retrospective using vintage photos, as well as brochures on new programs.

5. **Show videos or films in meeting rooms or auditoriums.** If you have new or existing films of your organization in action, show as many as possible in rooms.

6. **Ask visitors to sign a scrapbook or guestbook.** Have guestbooks for supporters to write good wishes for your organization's continued success. You will be able to use the remarks in future literature.

7. **Create a commemorative coin.** Design a metal coin with the dedication date and building silhouette. One side may have an inspirational message or your motto. Give the coin in small velour bags to all who attend.

77 Celebrating 50 Years

To celebrate 50 years in the field of scientific research, the Children's Hospital Oakland Research Institute (CHORI) of Oakland, CA, hosted a gala at the Chabot Space & Science Center (Oakland, CA). Jessika Diamond, interim special events manager, answers questions about the crowd-pleasing event:

Why was the venue of the Chabot Space & Science Center chosen for the event?

"Holding our party in a venue dedicated to science and education was a natural fit. The event began with scientific talks, furthering the theme."

What was unique about the gala?

"Our event was interactive — the reception took place just outside the Beyond Blastoff: Surviving in Space exhibit and we have pictures of guests trying out the interactive exhibits. They enjoyed defying gravity or pretending to be a shuttle repair crew member, and it added to the fun of the location, which added to the meaning of the event."

How else are you celebrating 50 years?

"We're holding a symposium in March 2010 at CHORI, featuring luminaries in related fields, including genetics, immunobiology, cancer and more discussing the latest discoveries and trends in their fields. Since no celebration of the past and present is complete without looking forward, we'll include talks and poster presentations from the young researchers at CHORI, the fellows and post-docs."

What tips can you share for marking a significant milestone at an organization?

"Use a milestone anniversary as an opportunity for a fundraising campaign.... Also, use this opportunity to blow your organization's horn about what's been accomplished over time. Use photos, retrospectives, histories and other ways that really promote why the organization has survived those five decades. Discussions of alumni, successes, achievements are also pertinent. You're essentially throwing a birthday party, and what birthday party doesn't focus on how wonderful the birthday boy/girl is?"

Source: Jessika Diamond, Special Events Manager (Interim), Children's Hospital & Research Center Foundation, Oakland, CA. Phone (510) 428-3885. E-mail: Jdiamond@mail.cho.org. Website: www.childrenshospitaloakland.org

78   Look to the Past for Great Stories About Your Organization

Compiling a detailed history of your organization will illustrate your organization's importance as it inspires and educates your current staff and supporters.

Staff at Villa Julie College (Owings Mills, MD) worked for two years to create a detailed history to commemorate the school's 60th anniversary.

In doing so, they sought to create more awareness and a sense of pride about the school, says Glenda LeGendre, vice president, marketing and public relations. The project was initiated by Kevin J. Manning, Ph.D., the college's president, and coordinated by a committee of three — LeGendre, the academic dean and a senior development office member.

Initally the committee sent a request for proposal (RFP) to three firms that produce and publish history texts. They chose History Associates Inc., which was located closest to the college and also in line with the budget allotted for this project.

Once they chose the printing company, the committee met to develop a recommended list of individuals for oral histories and to approve a timeline, LeGendre says.

"I then coordinated the project with the lead historian and tracked regular invoices/progress reports monthly," she says. "The other two committee members reconvened once more to assist with one round of edits and to help with the dedication page. Our president assisted with the dedication and epilogue ideas as well and also reviewed the final version."

The hardback book, "A Vision and A Promise: Villa Julie College", shown above, details the history, vision and growth of the college in 192 pages, five chapters and oral histories and photos of the past 60 years. Cost to produce each book was $18.

"The history firm worked on the research for about nine months and then the writing over the next four to five months," LeGendre says. "The editing process took perhaps two more months and probably four versions. Photo selection edits and cleanup took a fair amount of time. We improved on the scanned archival shots and identified other more current photos from our recent decade through my office."

They chose a Maryland-based printer who had skilled binding capabilities and does work for the Smithsonian and other quality print clients.

The book is currently being sold at the college's bookstore, and was first distributed to donors at a campaign kickoff event.

"We sent a copy of the book and a note to the historian writer at the *Baltimore Sun*, our main newspaper, but we

Vintage photographs are featured in this book, showcasing the 60-year history of Villa Julie College in Owings Mills, MD.

waited until after the campaign kickoff so the book would be a real surprise as an unveil," she says. "About 200 copies were distributed then; one per couple, and then another 75 distributed at our alumni reunion event during homecoming."

To continue to get the word out about the book, she says, "We're promoting its availability to alumni via e-mails and our magazine, to staff and faculty through other forums and to parents at exhibition booth setups at commencements."

One benefit of compiling a history of your organization is that it can unmask vital pieces of information. In Villa Julie's case, LeGendre says college officials had not known the exact date the college was founded until historians found a record stating the founding date was Oct. 1, 1947. With that knowledge in hand, she says, they plan to host a founder's day celebration on an annual basis.

Source: Glenda LeGendre, Vice President of Marketing & Public Relations, Villa Julie College, Owings Mills Academic Center, Owings Mills, MD. Phone (443) 352-4480.

79 ### Make Groundbreaking Magic

Launching a major building project? To maximize participation in your groundbreaking by the media and community:

- **Take an aerial photo of this major, memorable event.** Ask everyone attending to form a circle, holding hands if there are enough people, around the perimeter of the building's future walls. Instead of construction crews' stakes or flags, use colorful ribbons and posts. Your dignitaries can stand in the center to turn over the first shovels of dirt. Write a speech that promotes future hope and unity to be read by your speaker.

- **Start with the architect's rendering.** Use the drawing in press releases and a fundraising brochure with an envelope for pledges. Include facts of how the building will enhance services.

- **Ask supporters and employees to fill a time capsule.** A groundbreaking can be more fun with the burial of a time capsule full of items significant to your history.

Invite attendees to also sign a banner to put inside to involve them in this memorable event.

- **Invite a local or regional celebrity.** Ideally, this person will have some interest in your mission and be able to make brief remarks. Present him/her with a decorated shovel or hard hat and take plenty of photos for later use.

- **Pour a cement slab.** Then let attendees leave a thumbprint, their initials, a colorful stone or other memento. The slab can be set someplace inside or outside the new structure. Have soap, water, towels and lotion on hand for post-impression cleanup.

- **Hold an outdoor picnic.** Have a large tent, refreshments, games, speeches and even a contest for a facility name if one hasn't been chosen. Offer toy shovels for children and let them break ground themselves — a great photo opportunity!

 80 ### Tell Your Organization's Story Through Photos

Use images of your facilities, people and programs to tell the story of your cause.

Staff with the University of San Francisco (USF) of San Francisco, CA, created a 61-photo day-in-the-life slideshow for USF's print and online magazines.

"This was a fun way for our readers to experience a slice of life on campus," says Angie Davis, director of communications, USF School of Law and former editor of USF Magazine. "Many of our 80,000 readers, who are primarily alumni, haven't visited campus recently. We wanted to convey the vibrancy of our campus community, the diversity of our people and programs, how our mission is lived out on a daily basis, and just what it's like to spend a day on campus."

Two freelance photographers and one in-house photographer shot the images, taking a combined 1,400 photos in one day.

"We negotiated a standard full-day rate that included print and Web use of the photos," says Davis.

Planning which areas of campus would be photographed and at what times took roughly one month to coordinate. Doing so involved steps such as working with professors whose classes they wanted to photograph in action and determining where landscapers would be planting trees that day.

"I came up with a rough schedule of events and activities including classes, sporting events, lectures and rehearsals that were scheduled on the photo day, and I split up the assignments among the photographers," says Davis. "I also built in plenty of time for them to explore and roam the campus to capture the unplanned, spontaneous moments.

"Once the photos came back, I worked with our in-house team of four graphic designers to choose which photos to include in the magazine."

They shared the finished product in print and electronic versions of the magazine and on USF's intranet. Some photos shot during the day have been used in admissions brochures.

"We received very positive feedback from the campus community and readers, who said (the day-in-the-life feature) gave them a vivid picture of life at USF," says Davis. "One staff member told me it reminded him of why he is so proud to be a part of this university."

For organizations thinking of creating a photo story, Davis offers this advice, "The key is finding the right balance between having enough scheduled activities and events, and allowing enough free time for the photographers to use their own instincts in capturing spontaneous moments. I would recommend using photographers whose strength is in photojournalism."

Source: Angie Davis, Director of Communications, University of San Francisco, School of Law, San Francisco, CA. Phone (415) 422-4409.

81 Engage Supporters, Community With 'Name Our Mascot' Contest

Does your organization have a mascot or are you thinking of adding one? Host a contest to name the mascot to familiarize your supporters, community and local news media with the project while providing some great naming ideas.

Staff with Butler University (Indianapolis, IN) created a mascot-naming contest after people were confused about what to call the mascot, known simply as the Butler Bulldog, following a costume theft, says Lindsay Martin, manager, sports marketing & promotions.

"When our original costumes were stolen in August '08, there was some confusion among the news media and general public over what to call the bulldog costumes. Many were calling it Blue, which is actually the name of our live English bulldog mascot," says Martin. "That led to calls from fans thinking that the actual dog had been stolen. So we decided that by giving the costume a name of its own, we'd clear up any future confusion."

After two weeks of planning, they had the contest up and running. They publicized it first internally to faculty, staff and students via e-mail, then promoted it at basketball games, on the university website, on the mascot's Facebook page and on the live mascot's blog at www.butlerblue2.blogspot.com. They also publicized the contest to regional media outlets that covered the theft of the original costumes.

Community members submitted nearly 300 unique name suggestions online or in person at home basketball games. A nine-person committee (administrators from student affairs, university relations and athletics) narrowed this list down to a handful of entries. Fans then voted online and at basketball games for their favorite.

Officials announced the winning name, Hink, at a Jan. 22, 2009 men's basketball game, presenting the mascot with a team jersey emblazoned with the name.

The prize package for the four winners, all of whom submitted the name Hink, included four courtside seats to the game and a VIP experience with parking, programs and concessions. "We wanted a prize that was an experience, as opposed to just something they would put on a shelf," says Martin.

For organizations planning on creating a mascot naming contest, Martin recommends allowing the public to vote online as it will allow supporters far and wide to participate. In addition, she recommends narrowing down submissions to a handful of finalists that the public can choose from instead of letting them choose from a larger pool of random entries.

Source: Lindsay Martin, Manager, Sports Marketing & Promotions, Butler University, Hinkle Fieldhouse, Indianapolis, IN. Phone (317) 940-9468. E-mail: lmartin@butler.edu

Communications staff at Butler University (Indianapolis, IN) published results of a "Name Our Mascot" campaign with this website article.

Content not available in this edition

Lightning Source UK Ltd.
Milton Keynes UK
UKOW012318110713

213588UK00006BA/250/P

9 781118 691854